# Ways of Training

## Recipes for teacher training

**Tessa Woodward**

Pilgrims

Longman

**Longman Group UK Limited**
*Longman House, Burnt Mill, Harlow,*
*Essex CM20 2JE, England.*
*and Associated Companies throughout the world.*

This book is produced in association with Pilgrims
Language Courses Limited of Canterbury, England.

First published 1992

Set in 10/12 Cheltenham ITC Book

Produced by Longman Singapore Publishers (Pte) Ltd

Printed in Singapore

**British Library Cataloguing in Publication Data**
Woodward, Tessa
 Ways of Training: Recipes for Teacher
 Training
 I. Title
 407.1

ISBN 0-582-06493-7

**Illustrations**
Cover illustrated by John Barrett
Cartoons by Phillip Burrows

**Acknowledgements**
We are indebted to the following for permission to
reproduce copyright material: Cambridge University
Press for an extract from *Models and Metaphors in
Language Teacher Training* by Tessa Woodward
(1991); the authors, G Kenny and B Tsai for an extract
from *Sense of Teaching* (unpublished manuscript);
Pilgrims Publications for an extract by Tessa
Woodward from *The Teacher Trainer* Vol. 1/2, 1987;
Springer Verlag and the author for an extract from
*Oriental Stories as Tools in Psychotherapy* by N
Peseschkian (1986); TESOL for an adapted extract by
Tessa Woodward from 'Taking the stress out of
discussing lessons' in *TESOL France News*, Summer
1988.
We are grateful to the following for permission to
reproduce copyright material: The Bridgeman Art
Library for page 16 (left) and 16 (right); Oxford
University Press for page 87.

# A letter from the Series Editors

Dear Teacher,

This series of teachers' resource books has developed from Pilgrims' involvement in running courses for learners of English and for teachers and teacher trainers.

Our aim is to pass on ideas, techniques and practical activities which we know work in the classroom. Our authors, both Pilgrims teachers and like-minded colleagues in other organisations, present accounts of innovative procedures which will broaden the range of options available to teachers working within communicative and humanistic approaches.

We would be very interested to receive your impressions of the series. If you notice any omissions that we ought to rectify in future editions, or if you think of any interesting variations, please let us know. We will be glad to acknowledge all contributions that we are able to use.

*Seth Lindstromberg*
Series Editor

*Mario Rinvolucri*
Series Consultant

Pilgrims Language Courses
Canterbury
Kent
CT1 3HG
England

## Tessa Woodward

Tessa Woodward was raised in Devon and South Wales and took a degree at London University. She spent several years travelling, working in bars and restaurants and in more respectable jobs at the National Union of Students and the Martin Luther King Foundation before switching to EFL in the mid-seventies. She now works at Hilderstone College in Kent and edits *The Teacher Trainer* for Pilgrims. She also runs a British Council Specialist Course for teacher trainers. She has published *Loop Input* (Pilgrims), *Models and Metaphors in Language Teacher Training* (CUP), and articles in most main EFL periodicals. She recently gained an M.Phil in Education from Exeter University. She is married to Seth Lindstromberg who has managed to get her to slow down, work less and enjoy gardening and her horse, Peggy.

## Dedication

To Seth, Peggy and Emmett

# Contents

# List of activities

*'s-a'* indicates that either the main activity or a variation is suitable for *self-access* work
(in Chapter 5 it indicates suitability for self-access if trainees tape their own lessons)
* indicates that a process works best in the hands of a trainer with some counselling skills

# Acknowledgements

Thanks to Hilderstone College and, especially, Julie Parker, for providing me with steady work and an atmosphere conducive to making changes in courses.

Thanks to Seth, as ever, for his faith, his typing and for his editing too!

Thanks to all the people who read and commented on all or part of the manuscript: Mario Rinvolucri, Marion Cooper, Herbert Puchta, Janet Aitchison, Seth Lindstromberg, John Morgan, and Peter Grundy.

Thanks to Phillip Burrows for his great cartoons.

And thanks to all the teachers, trainers, trainees and language students I've worked with and from whom I've learned so much, and who have given me permission to record their ideas in this book.

# *Introduction*

## BACK TO THE BEGINNING

When I went out to work in Japan, over ten years ago, I found it very natural to share ideas with other teachers, to say what I thought, to swap books, to chat about a new technique, teacher to teacher. Later, still in Japan, when I was appointed in-service trainer, I expected to continue that same kind of 'working-with' teachers. On return from my Christmas holidays, however, ready to start my new job as trainer, I had a bit of a shock. Since business was rather slack, my boss had abruptly scheduled me to lead a two-week in-service training course for all the staff in January. Seeing my alarm at being asked to provide ten days of training, instantly, for my own colleagues, my boss compromised and said that we could all train each other. And that's exactly what we did.

Over the next two weeks I had a golden opportunity to watch my peers at work training each other. I also had the chance to learn more about my own training style. I saw David Reeves, fresh from an MA programme in California, introducing a neat plan for a skills lesson by drawing a diagram and speaking for just ten seconds. He then leant casually against the board and answered our shower of questions with an even more rapid hail of his own. Another day, I heard Ruth Kasarda declaring that she couldn't sit still a minute longer and saw her turning twenty jaded teachers into a lively, laughing crowd, trying out the ideas she wanted to share with us, all of which involved physical movement and fun. I saw teachers giving out stacks of paper, dividing people into pairs, refusing to explain, explaining without cease, using the floor, using the walls, walking out, and walking back in. It was a two-week crash course in input styles. And it was, I realise now, the start of this book.

Over the next six years, as I found myself not only doing in-house training but also running Royal Society of Arts Certificate and Diploma courses, giving presentations at workshops and conferences, and teaching on general refresher courses for teachers of all kinds, I searched for a handbook, for a list, for anything that could help me learn how to do teacher training better. I found a few manuals to help me with content, but apart from a booklet that is now out of print (UTMU 1976), a very short list of possible presentation modes for IATEFL conference presenters, and the odd article in, for example, Holden (1979) and British Council (1985), I could find almost nothing on the *process* of teacher training. So I decided to start making a pool of ideas for myself. I started with input styles but very soon widened my net to include ways of giving feedback, different ways of observing teachers and other areas as well. I watched others at work, interviewed them and asked people to tell me about their work. I adapted, collected and invented – and this book is the result. It represents a streamlined, public version of the huge mound of bits of paper and card that have been cascading out of box files at home for years.

## WHO IS THE BOOK FOR?

This book and the pool of ideas in it is for anyone who is interested in teacher training – trainee, trainer, organiser or administrator of training events. It is for people who help other people in staffrooms. It is for teachers who pop into each other's classrooms to team-teach or to observe each other. It is for groups of teachers who want to share ideas. It is for those with labels such as 'trainer', 'inspector' or 'assessor', as well as for others, perhaps 'heads of department', 'directors of studies' or 'school owners', who have some kind of training function within their jobs. It is also for those undergoing training, since it will enable trainees to see more clearly what their trainer's repertoire is and how this relates to their own learning preferences. It is also for course designers, since reading the book will help foster awareness of the variety of process types that could be used on any course you are designing.

Parts of the book may appeal to an even wider audience. For example, Chapter 2, *Input* is useful for anyone who has to give presentations or lectures of any kind. It would thus be useful to business people, to college lecturers, to speakers at women's institutes, to vicars. . .

It would be hard, of course, to cater for all these different groups within the instruction language of one book. I have therefore kept to the terms 'trainer' and 'trainee' throughout and I have written from the trainer's point of view. If you are a language teacher working in a group with other language teachers who are helping and training each other, then you are a trainer too (in the language of this book).

## TALKING ABOUT THE 'HOW' OF TRAINING

I've used the term *process* to discuss how learning and training events are structured. We do have a few special terms for different types of process. One such term is *lecture*. The lecture is usually taken to denote a time when one person speaks, usually with help from notes, and others listen, often writing things down. A lecture can be about anything – car maintenance, stable management or phonology. Lecturing is a process. It can convey many different kinds of content.

Another process term we have is *discussion*. We usually take this to mean a number of people sitting together, listening and talking about a particular issue or issues. The content (the issues and what is said about them) can be anything.

Another word we have to denote process is *brainstorm*. Here, a number of people think up as many ideas as possible around a particular topic in a non-judgmental way. A brainstorm can be about responses to naughtiness in cats, ways of indicating a language error, or anything else.

To recap, lectures, discussions and brainstorms are processes, or ways of structuring encounters. They are separate from content.

Lectures, discussions and brainstorms can either be short (two minutes) or long (an hour or more). Thus, they are also independent of time.

We do not have a great number of process terms, so in this book I have had to give my own names to many of the processes. (Sometimes I also refer to process types simply as 'ideas' or 'activities', but I always mean that part of an activity which is independent of content and time.)

Some people use the term (*mental*) *processing* to talk about what goes on in a person's mind when they are in a training/learning event. This is an interesting issue. It is not what I concentrate on in this book, however. I concentrate on the *external* structuring of training/learning events.

The term *process* denotes how encounters can be set up so that knowledge, skill or insight of trainees, trainers and others can be communicated between them. The process ideas in this book are thus about ways of enabling, sharing, eliciting, encouraging, questioning, responding, enriching and developing, as well as about more didactic 'transmission' actions such as telling, helping and informing.

Let's take the lecture, for example. We normally associate the process of lecturing with verbs such as *transmit* and *inform*. If we want a lecture to involve sharing, interacting, discussing or challenging, however, then we will need to change some steps in the normal lecture process (see ideas 2.1 to 2.15). For more on altering process ideas in order to fit different situations, see Chapter 1.

Regardless of content, a language teacher training course could conceivably stick totally to one process type, for example, the traditional lecture. This would fit the overall course model of 'the mug and jug' where the trainers are thought of as being full of wonderful knowledge that they pour into the empty trainees. A mug and jug course could also be run using more than one process type. For example, lectures could be supplemented with reading and very guided observation of experienced teachers. There would thus be three types of process used, all of which would be congruent with the mug and jug course model.

The course models that I tend to work with are 'the market place' (where everyone has something to offer and something to gain), 'the greenhouse' (where there is a protected environment and plenty of preparation for life outside) and 'the interactive circle' (where everyone learns from everyone else in a non-hierarchical way).

My personal preference is to use as wide a variety of process types as possible. But I need to make sure that the ones I choose are congruent with the overall course model I've chosen for that course. If I'm working in 'the greenhouse', I will need to use supportive processes early on. Choosing a process that forces trainees into 'spotlight' presentations or independent work too soon could startle a trainee who had been prepared for a warmer, softer initial environment.

Course models thus exert influence on process choices (see Woodward 1991). You might want to compare your own course models with mine. If they are radically different, then you may want to adapt the ideas here (see Chapter 1).

Process choices also exert an influence of their own – for example, on the atmosphere of a training room. Let's say that you choose, for example, an interactive, buzz-group lecture (2.5). When you try it out you'll find that your room is full of noise, questions, comments and contact between trainees. You will need to go along with this by withdrawing fully during buzz-group times and by being flexible with your material in order to deal with questions. You will need, generally, to accept a democratic environment. This may please you or not. One thing is certain – the choices you make in 'ways of training' will affect the atmosphere, role relationships and spirit of your course. It's important then that you should know more about the assumptions and philosophy behind the ideas here.

# THE BELIEFS AND ASSUMPTIONS BEHIND THIS BOOK

I will try to make clear, as far as I am aware of them, the beliefs behind the process ideas contained in this book. They represent my beliefs about teacher training.

## Training adults

As language teacher trainers, we are adults working with adults, be they eighteen-year-olds fresh from school or sixty-year-old headteachers switching fields. We are adults working with adults, and, thus, with our peers. The adults we work with will have memories of their own teachers and of their past learning experiences, be these happy memories or painful ones. Adults have minds that may be extremely active or which may not have been used much for a while. Adults are not just brains, but have bodies that need to move, eyes that need occasional visual feasts and imaginations that also need feeding.

Adults who come back into a classroom to learn to be teachers or to learn more about teaching ideas, are giving themselves a second chance at learning. They are giving learning a second chance too, a chance to prove that it can be stimulating, fun, and creative – a chance to prove that it can be a positive and dignified experience. And, if the second chance pays off, then, hopefully, some of the good in the experience will be passed on, in turn, to whoever they go on to teach.

## Becoming teacher trainers

Many of us don't have any real training as teacher trainers. We just drift into it, or are invited in, or barge our way in. What resources do we have to draw on? Memories of our own trainers and what they did, a few training manuals on content, the odd British Council specialist course if we've been lucky, a journal or two. When it comes to our training style – or *how* we run training sessions or courses – the chances are strong that we will be working from a small repertoire of process options that we have seen other people use. In my experience, people's repertoires tend to shrink when they are deprived of new information and stimulus, so it is probably accurate to say that many trainers are working with a shrinking stock of process options.

## Using a repertoire of process options

### ADVANTAGES FOR THE TRAINER
Once a trainer has a variety of different ways of doing the core tasks of their job, they can start to make choices as to which option to use according to whether they wish to:
– maximise a strength or minimise a flaw in their own training style,
– offer trainees a choice of process in sessions,
– find out which options harmonise or challenge trainee preferences, training aims, and so on,
– juggle or play with process options as a creative response to situational constraints.
Thinking about and making choices is a kind of personal research which can lessen boredom and add more personal meaning to a job.

### ADVANTAGES FOR TRAINEES
Trainees with different learning styles are better served on a course or at a session which has an inbuilt variety of process types or that offers a menu of process choices. Attending a course where a trainer is actively experimenting with process can lead, in turn, to trainees making energetic and thoughtful attempts to provide appropriate and varied process in classes with their own language learners.

Hearing and reading may be enough for some trainees, but others will need to participate, talk, draw, visualise, experience, chant, watch, and so on in order to truly take in and start to 'own' the new ideas offered to them. Thus, variety in training procedures may enable more trainees to learn than otherwise would be the case.

### THE EFFECT OUTSIDE THE TRAINING/LEARNING EVENT
Becoming aware of how things are done in training may lead us to become more aware of how things are done elsewhere – on television, in political speeches, in churches, in the theatre, in conversations, in journal writing. We may become more aware of what particular vehicle is being used, whether it is varied or monotone, whether it reinforces or works against the user's aims. This awareness can give us a whole other level to life. We will see much more when we look, hear much more when we listen, experience much more when we feel.

## Naming and categorising

Almost as soon as I had gathered ten or twenty process ideas, I began quite naturally, and without thinking, to name the ideas (e.g. ' Jim's snowstorm') and to put them into separate piles or categories. The names and categories have changed and evolved over the years I have worked with them, but they represent a sensible system, for me, and one that I can memorise and retrieve items from quickly and easily. As you try out a named idea, you may well find yourself calling it something else or you may want to classify it differently, in order to fit it in with your own personal schema and the process ideas that you use and know. This kind of personal naming, grouping and regrouping is an important way of getting to know and use an idea, adapt it and feel that it is in some way accessible, that it is your own. I hope that you will change the names, chapter headings, section order and anything else that you want to in this book. (For more on the theoretical rationale behind the whole book, see Woodward 1990.)

If your own beliefs about teacher training are extremely different from mine, there may be a lot of ideas in this book that you would not consider using. If, however, at least some of your beliefs about teacher training coincide with mine, then there may be a large number of ideas that you will feel comfortable with. Whatever your beliefs, as soon as you try out an idea, it will be filtered through your own personality and personal training style, will take place in a training event structured by its own parameters of training space, time, facilities, etc. and will be met by a unique group of trainees. In short, the idea will mutate as you use it. Ideas have a wonderful way of changing shape, too, as they are passed on from person to person in the form of advice and tips. After a few 'generations' of changes, as ideas are passed from trainer to trainer, they may change so much that they are virtually unrecognisable to the originator. I look forward to meeting, in the future, some of the ideas presented here and not recognising them!

## WHAT IS THE 'MAINSTREAM'?

Some early readers of this book thought that the ideas in it represented mainstream UK training. Others said the opposite. The reason for this, I think, is that trainers tend to feel that whatever *they* do is mainstream! I once met a trainer who often gave advice and feedback to teachers over the phone. He thought phone training was absolutely normal and mainstream.

I have stated my own preferred course models and some of my assumptions above. The best way for me to explain further how this book relates to the mainstream is to state the sort of training situations in which I have used the ideas in it. In the main, I have worked as a trainer with American, Canadian, Japanese and European teachers. I have only occasionally had the privilege of working with Indian, African or Soviet teachers. I have worked with only a few Chinese, South American and South East Asian teachers. I have not very often worked with groups larger than sixty. I have, though, worked with a range from complete novices right through to teachers with forty years of experience. The longest course I have worked on lasted two years, the shortest was forty-five minutes! As a trainer, I have worked with primary, secondary, tertiary and adult teachers, but my own experience does not include primary or secondary school teaching. I have worked on training courses that lead to certificates, diplomas and higher degrees and which involve reports, assessments and external exams, as well as on courses with no formal assessment at all. I was trained in the UK and have recently completed an MPhil here.

This may help you to see where adaptations might be necessary to suit your own situation. For more on adapting activities, see Section 1: 'Splitting the atom' in Chapter 1.

## HOW THIS BOOK IS ORGANISED

This book is structured around six core tasks of the job of teacher trainer. These six areas are the ones that I saw as most important when I started collecting ideas and are the subject of Chapters 2 to 7. Chapter 1 is intended to help you to analyse the ideas in the rest of the book so that you can adapt them and create new ideas for your own training situation.

Chapters 2 to 7 are not in chronological order of use or in order of importance. In other words, simply because *Input* is the first of these chapters, it does not follow that it is the most important or that you should use these ideas first. Ideally, the chapters could be arranged in a circle, so that they could all be seen as equally important and all usable in any order. Circles are hard to combine, however, with books that are read from front to back. After trying the chapter order out on many different readers, I decided to put *Input* first only because it was the block of work that made the notion of 'process' clearest to those who had not considered the concept much before.

## THE RECIPE HEADINGS

Each individual process idea is written up under the following headings: 'Materials', 'Trainees', 'Procedure', 'Variations', 'Rationale/Comment' and 'Acknowledgements/Reading'. These headings are largely self-explanatory. Occasionally, information for the user is given under additional headings such as 'Time in the course' (e.g. 'near the end') and 'Content' (e.g. 'dense, with definite, separate sections').

'Variations' is an important heading as it highlights possible adaptations to the main idea. These adaptations can make an idea usable in your own situation where the main idea is not. The variation may seem to differ only slightly from the main idea, but may radically change the atmosphere of a training/learning session and open up further paths and options.

Under the 'Rationale/Comment' heading I give reasons for trying out the process idea, and there is often a discussion of aims too. The danger in this is that the rationale I give might disguise the usefulness to you of an idea if your aims are different. Thus, the remarks under the 'Rationale/Comment' heading will give you an idea of why *I* would choose to use that particular process idea. It is not a guarantee of success in achieving that aim, however – there are too many other factors involved, not least, the trainees' and language students' aims.

Any process recipe usable by trainees working on their own is marked '*s-a*', for 'self-access' in the List of activities on pages vi–vii.

Virtually all the processes described are ones I've tried, tested and adapted many times. I can say of all the ideas that they work for me. There are one or two that require a warmed-up group, or a group of people who feel fairly comfortable with each other. These last activities also require a flexible, sensitive trainer who has some counselling skills.

I was wondering at one stage whether to put a 'Government Health Warning', playfully, on a couple of exercises. But, then again, that could put people off activities that work excellently if handled with tact. Besides, I might not label the right processes for you. You will see processes differently for your circumstances than I will for mine. So, as a compromise, in the List of activities, I have marked with an asterisk those which I think will work better if the trainer is flexible, experienced, sensitive and has some counselling skills.

## DIFFERENT WAYS OF USING THIS BOOK

Apart from manipulating the book physically (e.g. cutting it up into cards kept in a box or spread out on a table), you might like to consider the following ways of using it:

1 Skim through, reading in each chapter only the introduction and a few of the recipes in Chapters 2 to 7. This will give you a fast overview of some of the core tasks in teacher training.

2 Carefully read one of Chapters 2 to 7 all the way through, along with its introduction. This will give you plenty of ideas for one part of the job.

3 Read the chapter that corresponds to the area that you are *worst* at. You may find the start of a new approach.

4 Choose a few ideas that appeal to you, try them out, write up your own comments on them, do the follow-up reading, and generally consider the variations, advantages, disadvantages, effects, and reasons for one idea in depth. You may well then want to add your own variations to and improvements on the idea.

**5** Read Chapter 1 first.

**6** Think about matching the process ideas to factors such as your own mood, personality, different learning styles, different training parameters – such as size of room, length of course, different content types or other variables.

Running matching experiments of this kind and keeping a log of them, a kind of 'process diary', can be interesting work. Imagine, for example, that trainees have expressed a feeling of being overloaded. You might record their comments and your own feelings about them. You could then deliberately slow down, select process options that allow for recall, review, consolidation and reflection time, and record reactions to these from trainees and yourself. (For more on process experiments of this kind, see Woodward 1990.)

**7** Start a chapter of your own, on a training area that has not been included in this book, for example, 'interviewing' or 'assessing teachers'.

**8** Think about which combinations of ideas go together well, giving similar messages to course participants. Then, think about the process ideas which, when combined on a course or in a session, would give radically different, even jarring or incongruous messages, to participants. For example, letting each trainee negotiate the type of assignment they wish to do yet then marking them all by the same inflexible and hidden code of grades could create a feeling of dissonance on a course.

**9** Think about which ideas are congruent with your overall course model or course aims. Which ideas actually work *against* your own aims and course models?

There are no doubt many other ways of using this book that I have not thought of. The ideas above are merely suggestions to start you off!

## STYLISTIC NOTE

I use contractions freely throughout. This allows uncontracted forms to serve their natural function of signalling emphasis, as in *do not* versus *don't*.

The pronoun *she* is used frequently to refer to the individual trainer, trainee, teacher or student. This is because I feel it makes a nice change for women to see themselves in texts. It will also have an effect on men readers which they may like to reflect upon.

# CHAPTER 1

# *Making this book work for you*

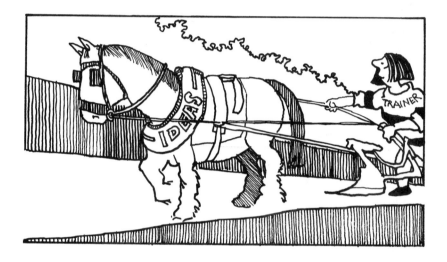

## *Section 1: Splitting the atom*

When I meet an idea that I like, I have a strong tendency to try it out almost exactly as I met it. I may make a few minor changes but generally I tend to copy or imitate by doing what I saw being done, or read, or heard about. It feels safer to do that. 'I saw it work so I can make it work for me' is perhaps the feeling I have at first. It's only after I've gained confidence with the idea and got it firmly into my repertoire that I start to play with it and introduce changes.

You may find you have the same tendency in using the ways of training in this book. At first sight some may make you feel, 'No, I couldn't use that. It's not me'. Others may tempt you and you may find yourself trying them out exactly as they are described. To show you how to get more mileage out of *these* ideas and to encourage you to try the ones that *don't* appeal at first sight, I offer the following framework. I've nicknamed it 'Splitting the atom', since it involves breaking training processes down into 'components'. In Woodward (1988f) this framework was applied to language learning activities. Here, it is adapted for the training classroom.

## Step 1

Try out any training process in the book as a trainee would so that you are completely clear about all the steps, the necessary materials, organisation of participants, and so on.

## Step 2

Analyse the process in detail. There are many different ways of doing this. Here are just nine areas to consider:

**a** Organisation – How are the people and the furniture arranged?

**b** Materials – What is needed by the trainer, and by the trainees?

**c** Time – What preparation time is involved before class? Roughly how long does the process last in class the way *you* use it? Is any follow-up time desirable or necessary?

**d** Procedure – What do the trainees do? What does the trainer do?

**e** Level/Type – As the activity stands, what level or type of trainees and trainer is it good for?

**f** Before and After – What could happen the minute/session/week before the activity? Any useful follow-ons?

**g** Topic – Is there any particular subject or theme implied? Or is the process applicable to almost any content?

**h** Beliefs – What beliefs about learning, people, language or training are implied by the process? For example, a standard lecture would imply, amongst other things, that people learn well from listening to someone else speak at length, that intake roughly equals input, that people will be able to remember, understand and apply the information gained in the lecture.

**i** Reasons – This is the most important component, and involves asking yourself why a process is used at all.

## The grammar of training processes: Analysis of an example process

Once you have completed Steps 1 and 2, you have a description, or recipe, that will allow you to reproduce that process any time you want. To illustrate this analysis, let's take the idea of the 'brainstorm' and consider its components.

### THE BRAINSTORM

**a** Organisation

Trainees are seated in plenary facing towards the main public writing space (e.g. the board or flipchart).

**b** Materials

A large writing space such as a board.

**c** Time

No preparation time is necessary. In class, approximately five to ten minutes. Follow-up time will vary depending on what the brainstorm is used for.

**d** Procedure

The trainer selects a central theme. Trainees call out spontaneously and rapidly ideas connected to the central theme. The trainer writes these onto the board without comment in a random array.

**e** Level or type of trainee and trainer

Trainees: Any, since the theme is chosen to suit the trainees you have. Trainer: One who can be non-judgmental of trainees' ideas.

**f** Before

Trainees do some thinking or reading to prepare for the brainstorm.

After

The brainstorm can be followed by further input in the form of discussion and/or prioritisation of the items gathered or, alternatively, by groupwork, homework or by a lecture.

**g** Topic

Any.

**h** Beliefs

Trainees like working in plenary. Ideas, if not judged or assessed, will flow freely. It's easier for people to think of ideas if they don't have to prioritise them at the same time. Seeing and hearing other people's thoughts triggers more of one's own. It's OK for the trainer to be a silent scribe. You do not need to take a position on everything that comes from trainees.

**i** Reasons

To find out what trainees know/remember/associate with a particular theme. To share the initial thoughts of the group publicly so people can see who knows/thinks what. To tune a group into a topic. For review.

## Step 3: Creating new training processes from the process you've analysed

As it stands, the brainstorm is a whole-class calling-out and writing-up activity. By altering as little as one detail in one of the components above, a radically different process can be created.

Let's change some details of the first component, 'organisation'. Instead of sitting in plenary, trainees sit in groups working with a separate board in each group. Immediately the room is a little noisier and several scribes are involved. Inevitably, people look at other groups' boards and see the brainstorms on them developing in, possibly, very different ways. This adds an extra stimulus to their thoughts.

Next, let's change a detail of the 'materials' component. Instead of using a large board, ask trainees to do the brainstorm into their own notebooks. There is now a very quiet atmosphere. Trainees have their heads down, saying little or nothing.

Now, what about 'before and after'? If we change the timing so that the brainstorms are created by trainees *before* they come to the session, then, *in* the session, trainees can compare their own brainstorms with other people's and add interesting points from other people's notes onto their own. Or, we can add a step to the end. That is, once the random array has gone up on a large board, each trainee prioritises or categorises the points that have come up, thus breaking the theme down into areas or sequences. This creates a two-step process. One is whole-group, fast and sociable, the second is quiet, thoughtful and slower.

If we change the 'reasons' component and decide to do a brainstorm to *test* trainees, this could lead us to give out handouts to trainees. On the handout would be an incomplete brainstorm with, for example, spaces left for some writing as in Figure 1. The trainees' task is to fill in the gaps and/or to use the brainstorm as a prompt either for discussion with others, or for a short essay.

If we made changes to different components or different changes to these components, we would come up with many additional, different ways of brainstorming.

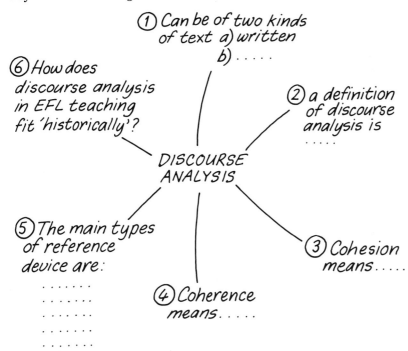

Fig. 1 Handout of incomplete brainstorm

## The advantages of 'splitting the atom' and changing the components

Looking at a training process in detail, analysing it into components and then changing details of the components has a number of advantages:
- It helps us to know the idea more thoroughly, to remember it, to want to try it out and to create our own variations.
- Instead of an immediate reaction such as 'I could never use that in my training room', it encourages us to see that process ideas can be adapted to fit the circumstances.

- If a training process seems to imply a lot of noise, we can change it so that it's quiet.
- If an idea involves too much space, we can change it to suit our smaller room.
- If it is designed to suit an aim we don't agree with, we can rewrite it to suit our aims.

In short, 'splitting the atom' encourages ideas to mutate. It makes a little go a long way.

## Section 2: The options approach

I take the word *option* from Earl Stevick's *Images and Options in the Language Classroom* (1986). From that book I gained the idea that every time a teacher walks into a classroom a range of options opens up in front of her. She can say 'Hello!' to the class, or go straight to the board, or talk to a student or do many other things. Each option has its advantages and disadvantages. Going straight to the board to draw something may get everyone's attention in a quiet, undemanding way, but it may also make some students feel cheated of a greeting. Whichever option is chosen initially will, in turn, open up a further range of options. So, standing at the board, drawing, a teacher can choose whether to draw silently, ask the students what they think is being drawn, or ask students to come up and join in with the drawing. Any of these options has built-in advantages and disadvantages and in turn opens up new ranges of further options. (Diagrammatically, this might look like Figure 2, from Woodward 1988c.) Similarly, at any moment in a training room, a trainer has choices before her and each one will have its advantages and disadvantages and be right in some way and certainly be right *at some time*.

In this book I have tried to provide a large variety of ways of training. By applying your own ideas and by 'splitting the atom', you can add greatly to the number of options available to us.

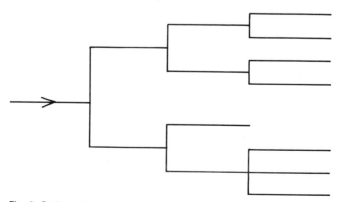

Fig. 2 Options diagram

# Section 3: What to do with the options: An appetiser

There was a pre-service trainee once. A tall, friendly fellow with a habit of standing and sitting extremely close to some of his young, shy Japanese women students. He worked *so* closely to them that they shrank more and more into the backs of their chairs, lowering their heads, avoiding his gaze. They looked a picture of embarrassment and practically gave up speaking altogether.

Others in his training group chatted to him about cultural differences in eye contact, physical proximity and so on. No change! I tried counting the number of unanswered questions he asked the Japanese women and asking the trainee why he thought the questions went unanswered. No change!

Finally, I hit on a fresh option. I drew some swift pictures of his position in the classroom one day (see Figure 3). He looked at the pictures aghast. 'Do I *really* get that close?' he asked. We all replied, 'Yes!' He changed.

*Presentation*

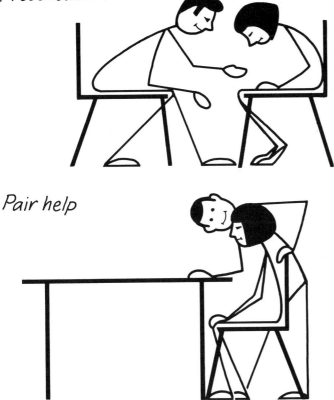

*Pair help*

Fig. 3

# CHAPTER 2

# *Input*

My first sermon                    My second sermon

'*Wenn alles schläft und einer spricht, dass nennt der Lehrer Unterricht.*'
Swiss proverb   (When everybody's sleeping and one person's speaking,
then that's what the teacher calls *teaching*.)

The word *input* comes from the world of systems engineering. It
highlights the content being 'put in' and rather downplays the recipient
of that content. Other terms such as *content*, *course components*,
*teaching*, or *training* also tend to emphasise 'transmission', that is,
information or knowledge being passed from one who knows to one who
doesn't. This works against the idea that everyone in a group has
knowledge and experience inside them and that everyone present,
including the trainer, can learn from a training encounter. These terms
hide the following:

- Content, no matter how it arrives in a session, has to be worked on,
  reacted with and processed by participants.
- Intake is very rarely the same as input.
- The fact that something is taken in by an individual does not mean
  that there will necessarily be an output.
- If there is an output, it is as unpredictable as intake.

Thus, the term *input* sounds a lot neater and simpler than real-life
learning and training actually is.

This section includes ideas for eliciting and transmitting information, ideas, opinions and awarenesses in teacher-training sessions from and to all those present at the learning event. It aims to bring into light some of the options obscured by current terminology and viewpoints. If you would like to discover something about your own attitudes to 'input' or your own current training practice in input sessions, you can do the task that follows.

## PRE-TASK: INPUT QUESTIONNAIRE

After you have finished an input sessions for pre- or in-service teacher trainees, you might like to think about these questions:

1 What were your main content aims in the session?
2 What methods or vehicles did you use to bring the input into the session? A lecture? A handout? Questions? Groupwork? Posters? Others?
3 Did you deliberately choose these processes for the session from among a range of options in your repertoire or would you say that they were a combination that you quite often use without too much thought about alternatives?
4 If you chose your process methods carefully, from a broad repertoire, what criteria did you use for their selection?
5 Looking back after the session, how appropriate do you think the processes were for your particular group, input, and situation, and for individual trainees in the group?
6 Did you like using these process types?
7 Where and when did you first learn how to use them?
8 Since then, have you had the time, opportunity or inclination to read about, think about or discuss input processes?
9 Do you feel you would know where to get information on these or other process types if you wanted to?
10 Do you know of any other ways, or processes, for introducing input to a group? Could you make a list of them?
11 Have you ever seen any of the ones you have listed being used?
12 If not, where did you find out about them?
13 Are there any other process ideas you have never seen but can imagine might work? Given the perfect circumstances and enough time, money and so forth, are there any imaginative new ways that you would like to try?
14 Did you make any notes for the session when planning it? If so, have a glance at them. What percentage of the notes apply to content and what to process?

### OTHER WAYS OF USING THIS QUESTIONNAIRE

a Video or sound tape your input session. Play the tape back and *then* think about the questions.

**b** Ask a colleague to sit in on a session and then get her to ask you the questions in an interview.

**c** Sit in on a colleague and do the same for them.

N.B. If used between colleagues, it is vital that the questionnaire is *not* used to assess or evaluate the person questioned. Under a threat of this kind, most trainers will act like normal human beings, that is, they will give fashionably 'right' answers and little will be learned by either party.

READING
'Styles of EFL Teacher Trainer Input' (Woodward 1989c).

# Section 1: Lectures

When we think of a 'lecture', we usually think of one person standing in front of a class of students sitting in rows. The lecturer talks. The class listens and writes notes; and there may be a handout. This section on lectures offers other ways of structuring the process of a lecture: ways which give new roles for the listener and lecturer and even for the handout!

## Listener's role

We usually think of the listener's role in a lecture as being rather passive. We think of rows of people listening to one voice and mentally sifting or mentally drifting. Some variations implied in this section are:
**1** Trainees listen in order to:
  - see if the lecturer agrees or disagrees with a particular statement (2.3 *Lecture discussion scales*);
  - recap the lecturer's ideas as faithfully as possible (2.4 *The Curran-style lecture*);
  - recap, question, comment and predict from small amounts of input (2.5 *The buzz-group lecture*);
  - see how the lecturer defines a particular item of terminology (2.7 *Lecture key words*);
  - listen to other trainees (2.3 *Lecture discussion scales*, 2.4 *The Curran-style lecture*, 2.5 *The buzz-group lecture* and 2.12 *Participant mini-lectures*).
**2** The lecturer listens to the trainees (2.4 *The Curran-style lecture*, 2.5 *The buzz-group lecture*, 2.7 *Lecture key words*, 2.12 *Participant mini-lectures*).

## Lecturer's role

It is important that the lecturer, when listening to comments, questions, summaries and so on, should (a) be non-judgmental in expression, gesture and word, (b) be interested in answering trainees' questions and not pose as devil's advocate to the poor questioner, (c) allow time for the questioner's point to be made without interruption and, (d) if necessary, allow herself time to restate the question for clarification. (See Rinvolucri 1985.)

The processes given in this section open out the lecturer's role to allow:
- expression of agreement and disagreement by the trainees (2.3 *Lecture discussion scales*);
- the lecturer rest and reflection time (2.4 *The Curran-style lecture*, 2.5 *The buzz-group lecture* and 2.10 *Listen, read and rest*);
- the lecturer a chance to listen to trainees (the above processes plus 2.11 *The backwards lecture*, and 2.12 *Participant mini-lectures*);
- the lecturer to reorganise prepared material (2.5 *The buzz-group lecture*);
- the trainees to give feedback on what's been understood (2.4 *The Curran-style lecture*, 2.5 *The buzz-group lecture* and 2.9 *The interactive, or interrupted lecture*);
- trainees to give feedback on lecturer style (2.14 *Instant questionnaire feedback*);
- everyone to tell stories and anecdotes (2.2 *Story starters*).

## The handout

Usually, we think of a handout as being prepared by the lecturer in advance of a talk as a list of the main points made by the speaker, used by the speaker as a prompt during the talk and, finally, given out to the audience as they leave.

This section gives interesting variations to this:
- The lecturer, using a more interactive style, (e.g. in 2.5 *The buzz-group lecture*) will need to wait until after the session to write up a handout, as she will not know beforehand exactly which points will come up.
- In the case of 2.7 *Lecture key words*, it is the group that produces the handout, during the discussion. It is a summary of their own input and is simply affirmed or corrected by the lecturer.
- When using 2.3 *Lecture discussion scales*, the group sits together after the lecture and pools the main points and the finer details and so makes their own group handout.
- 2.8 *Socratic questioning* involves trainees in writing their own handouts after the session, at home. Prompted by the socratic questions on the worksheet, they note down the results of the discussion.
- 2.12 *Participant mini-lectures* involves the lecturer in making the hand outs from notes, comments, corrrections, and queries made by trainees during the session.
- A handout doesn't have to consist of prose. It can contain diagrams, mind maps, key words, multiple-choice questions, true/false statements, texts to be corrected or adapted, or texts and text headings all run together (thathavetoberewrittenseparatedandarrangedtoshowmain

andminorpoints) or jumbled statements that have to be sequenced properly.
– A handout doesn't have to be complete. It can be half-filled in.
– A handout doesn't have to be given out at the end. It can be given out at the beginning for participants to correct, sequence or fill out during the lecture.

## 2.1

**MATERIALS**
None

**TRAINEES**
Any

**TRAINER**
Experienced,
flexible, sensitive

# LISTENER DEFENCES
## Procedure

1 Give a little bit of your lecture and then stop.
2 Invite participants to comment on all the ways they have been defending themselves from your lecture. For example, some people may have been working on shopping lists or private letters while also taking notes on your lecture. Others may have written notes to people around them. Some people may have stopped to think about something you said earlier in the lecture, thus taking the risk of missing out on later points. Other listeners may have started to drift off into a trance, staring vaguely at the back of the person in front of them or doodling on their notepads.
3 Discuss with the group all the strategies you usually use to win back their attention to the point you wish them to be concentrating on. Tell them about the way you sometimes insert sudden questions or tasks, tell jokes or anecdotes, reinforce points visually on the board or throw in puzzles or provocative statements.
4 Together with participants, explore new ways a listener can stay creative during lectures.

**RATIONALE/COMMENT**
This type of discussion can make overt the fact that lecturers attempt to dominate their listeners' attention and that the listeners may or may not want that to happen. It can open up a discussion of the traditional lecture from both the giver's and receiver's point of view and can be the starting point for suggestions by the lecturer and listener about other ways of lecturing that are less dogmatic or one-way.

ACKNOWLEDGEMENT
My thanks to Mario Rinvolucri for this one.

# STORY STARTERS

## Procedure

**2.2**

**MATERIALS**
A story

**TRAINEES**
Any

1 Start off the session by telling an anecdote, parable or story that is related to the theme of the session. For instance, 'How I became a teacher', 'A lesson that went disastrously wrong' or 'How I feel when there's an observer in my classroom'.
2 Trainees can ask questions, comment or be silent.
3 Invite them to add anecdotes of their own on the same subject.

**VARIATION**
The stories can also be told at the end or in the middle of a session.

**RATIONALE/COMMENT**
a Anecdotes are fairly easy to tell, and they give participants a chance to learn something about the lecturer.
b 'Anecdotes are non-threatening, engaging, memorable and foster independence as the individual needs to make their own sense out of the message' (Jeffrey Zeig, quoted in Rosen 1982 p.33). So, it can actually be a good thing if your anecdote is a little oblique or is not on exactly the same subject as the main topic of the session.

Sample anecdotes

*1*

In an adult language learning class one day, the (native-speaking) teacher held up a picture from a magazine. She said:
T   Does anyone know what this is?
S   Yes, it's a painting by Dali. Name is 'Sleep'.
T   Gosh! Well done, Maria. You knew that!
As soon as the teacher had said this the student blushed and fell silent. The teacher went on, 'Now I want you to name all the things you can see in the picture. Maria?' But Maria was silent. She would not speak.

*2*

The mullah, a preacher, entered a hall where he wanted to give a sermon. The hall was empty except for a young groom seated in the front row. The mullah, pondering whether to speak or not, finally said to the groom, 'You are the only one here. Do you think I should speak or not?' The groom said to him, 'Master, I am but a simple man and do not understand these things. But, if I came into the stables and saw that all the horses had run off and only one remained, then I would feed it nevertheless.'

The mullah took this to heart and began to preach. He spoke for over two hours. After that he felt elated and wanted his audience to confirm how great his sermon had been. He asked, 'How did you like my sermon?' The groom answered, 'I told you already that I am a simple man and do not understand these things very well. However, if I came into the stables and found all the horses gone except one I would feed it, but I wouldn't give it all the fodder I had.' (Peseschkian 1986)

## 2.3

**MATERIALS**
Slips of paper with
statements and
scales on,
photocopied (or
written out) and
cut up

**TRAINEES**
Any; this is
especially helpful
to non-native
speaker trainees

# LECTURE DISCUSSION SCALES

## Preparation

1 Pick out the central points from a talk you want to give. Write them down as provocative statements that can be agreed or disagreed with. For example, a talk on translation may touch on ten main issues. Changed into arguable statements, they could be:
  - Translation is unfashionable in language teaching but it is a very natural activity.
  - The best texts to translate are those written by famous authors.
  - Every word or phrase is translatable into the target language.
  - There is no one perfect translation for a particular word in a language.
  And so on.

2 Write or type your statements and, under each, draw a line or scale like this:

*agree* ⟵————————————⟶*disagree*

3 Photocopy your sheet of statements and scales and cut them into strips.

## Procedure

1 Give one statement and scale to each person.
2 Everyone reads their own statement slip first, thinks about it and then marks the scale with an X according to whether and how much they agree or not. This one, for instance, shows quite strong agreement:

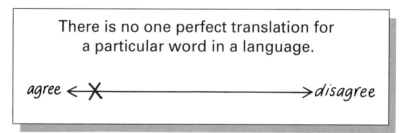

There is no one perfect translation for
a particular word in a language.

*agree* ⟵—X————————————⟶*disagree*

3 Trainees now mill around telling the others what is on their slip and how they feel about it. They try to find someone who agrees with their statement to the same extent. There will naturally be some discussion. Once all the participants have spoken to several others, ask them to sit down.
4 Give your talk.
5 While listening, people will tend to focus especially well on the part of the talk that deals with 'their' issue. They may be interested to know the position *you* take.

**6** After the lecture, encourage the group to pool the key points. Or finish your talk a bit early and leave the group to this open-ended discussion. There is a good chance that individuals will have strong recall of the points of the lecture referred to on their own slips of paper.

### RATIONALE/COMMENT

**a** This idea is particularly useful for times when content goes against established opinions.

**b** The initial reading, thinking and talking focuses attention on the subject, making people aware of what information or opinions they have on the theme.

**c** People can relax and enjoy the lecture knowing they have, between them, already got the key points.

**d** By meeting afterwards and comparing the slips with what they remember from the talk, people can see if you omitted any points you had planned to include. These points can be jointly researched and presented by trainees next time.

ACKNOWLEDGEMENT/READING
I learnt the main idea from Cynthia Beresford. (See Woodward 1987b.)

# THE CURRAN-STYLE LECTURE
## Procedure

**1** Before starting your talk, ask for two volunteers to help you. Explain that there is no test involved. They will be acting as mirrors or sounding boards so that you can know how successful or not your talk has been. They can bring a pen and paper if they wish.

**2** Ask them to sit slightly behind you, one to your left, one to your right.

**3** Start the first section of your lecture and stop after a few minutes.

**4** Gently ask one of your helpers to explain to you what she thinks she heard. Use language such as, 'What did you understand of my mini-lecture?' or 'Can you tell me what you think my main points were?' rather than 'What can you remember?' Also say, 'That's interesting! I couldn't have explained that very well' rather than 'You got that wrong!' In other words, avoid judgmental, blocking language. While she is talking, listen closely to see if she has missed or misunderstood anything important.

**5** If she has, you have the chance to explain again.

**6** Ask your second helper, 'Is there anything you'd like to add?' or 'Was that your impression too?'

**7** After your helpers have recapped and you have dealt with any misunderstandings or omissions, go on to the next section of your talk. Again, stop after a few minutes and this time ask the second helper to start recapping first. Go through your whole talk this way.

## 2.4

**MATERIALS**
None

**TRAINEES**
This process is especially good for non-native speaker trainees since everyone gets a second chance at everything

**CONTENT**
This process works best with a challenging and intensive lecture

## VARIATIONS

**a** Helpers stay in their own seats in the audience.

**b** Different helpers volunteer after a few sections.

**c** You suggest who should be the helpers.

**d** Some trainees prefer the helpers to be appointed before a section of the lecture so that they personally can 'switch off' if they are not called on. Others prefer the helpers to be chosen after sections of the talk since this helps everyone to keep on their toes.

**e** An extremely simple version of *The Curran-style lecture* consists of merely asking the group, at the end of the lecture, 'Well, what did you learn?' and waiting for a gradual response from different group members.

## RATIONALE/COMMENT

**a** The lecture is broken down into short sections.

**b** The audience hears a variety of voices.

**c** People experience different feelings when just listening than when listening to recap. For example, some may tend to lose concentration when they are under the stress of knowing that they will shortly be asked to recap what they are hearing. Others find that having a motivation like this actually helps them concentrate.

**d** You switch from speaking to very attentive listening.

**e** You can tell how much of your message has been understood and remembered.

**f** Everyone sees how different people are in what they take in.

**g** This process really helps the lecturer who is bursting to tell all she knows about a subject to slow down, stop and check with learners how much they understand.

READING
Curran (1972 and 1976) and Woodward (1987c).

## 2.5

**MATERIALS**
None

**TRAINEES**
Any, but especially non-native speaker trainees

**CONTENT**
This process works best with a challenging and intensive lecture

# THE BUZZ-GROUP LECTURE

## Procedure

1 Seat the audience so that later they can work in 'buzz' groups of two to six. Give people time to say 'hello' to others in their group.

2 Work out a signal for stopping the groups, and demonstrate it so everyone knows what to expect.

3 Give the first few minutes of your talk.

4 Stop and ask people to work in their buzz groups and quickly recap orally on what they think they heard or understood.

5 At your pre-arranged signal, the buzz groups stop buzzing. Continue with the next section of your talk, before stopping again and allowing the buzz groups to work.

### VARIATIONS IN THE BUZZ-GROUP TASK

**a** Trainees work together to restate your main points and make sure everyone in their buzz group has them noted down correctly.

**b** Trainees prepare one question or comment on the talk so far.

**c** Different buzz groups note down different things, e.g. one group notes down advantages and another disadvantages, or some other category of distinction relevant to the lecture.

**d** For 'silent buzzing', pairs of trainees simply swap notes after each section of the lecture.

### VARIATIONS IN WHAT THE LECTURER DOES DURING BUZZ-GROUP TIME

**a** You stay at the front to allow buzz groups to work without interference.

**b** You go around eliciting the questions and comments produced during the buzz-group work. If these have been written down, collect the bits of paper.

**c** You keep these questions and comments until the end of the talk or use them as a basis for recapping, straightening out misunderstandings or structuring the rest of the talk as you go along.

### RATIONALE/COMMENT

**a** In this process participants have a chance to restate lecture content, ask questions and offer comments, thus developing oral and recall skills, and confidence and flexibility with the subject matter. This is especially good for non-native speaker trainees since they have more than one chance to catch things and plenty of opportunity to find out from peers whether they have understood or not.

**b** Participants interact both with content and with people. They express doubts and questions as a group rather than as brave, but scared individuals in a crowd.

**c** You gain instant feedback on the level of audience comprehension and interest.

**d** You are forced to think in manageable chunks of content, and to be responsible and flexible. This helps you to feel more awake and less isolated.

ACKNOWLEDGEMENTS/READING
I first learnt this technique from Mario Rinvolucri, and I first learnt variation (c) of the buzz-group task from Alan Matthews and Sheila Estaire. See Brown (1978 p. 51) and Woodward (1987d).

# PRE-LECTURE UNFINISHED SLIPS

## Preparation

**1** Prepare, on slips of paper, a class set of unfinished statements or questions for trainees to complete. The statements can be designed either to help participants to get to know each other ('The name of

**2.6**

**MATERIALS**
Slips of paper

**TRAINEES**
Any

the person on my left is . . .'), to settle into the atmosphere ('I feel . . . at the moment' or 'The lecturer looks a bit . . .'), or to review past material ('I remember three important things from our last lecture on semantics. These are: 1. . . 2. . . 3. . .') or a mixture of all three.

2 Put one copy of the statements on each chair before people arrive.

## Procedure

1 As trainees come in, they will tend to pick up the slips, read them and complete them. If they don't, encourage them to do so, perhaps by leaving a message on the board.
2 Allow time for participants to complete the slips.
3 People compare their filled in slips with each other.
4 Start the lecture.

### EXTENSION

5 At the end of the lecture, ask each participant to write a new pre-lecture unfinished slip for the topic of your next lecture. Take these in for use next time.

Or, ask them to write slips which review the session they have just heard, perhaps thus, 'The five main points in the lecture on "setting student homework" were . . .' Ask them what they have written and discuss this before moving on to new content.

### VARIATION

Different slips bear different statements or questions so that different trainees work on different things.

### RATIONALE/COMMENT

a This process gives trainees something to do if they arrive early.
b It gives you time to prepare your boardwork or get your session materials ready while trainees are working with the slips.
c If the slips bear questions about past content, this can be a useful way of organising review.

ACKNOWLEDGEMENT
I first learnt this technique from Jean-Paul Creton.

## 2.7

## LECTURE KEY WORDS

### Preparation

**MATERIALS**
A few key words from your next lecture written on slips of paper and duplicated for all participants

**TRAINEES**
Any

1 Choose four or five words or phrases that are central to your topic and write them down. Make a class set of this list. The terms can either be new field-specific vocabulary items or simply words encapsulating the key points.
2 Give the list out to trainees either just before the lecture or some days prior to it.
3 Trainees research the words, discuss their associations and meanings and, from this, try to predict the content of the session.

## Procedure

1 Give your talk. As each term arises, invite participants to explain its meaning and relevance to the context.
2 Give them time to note down any differences between their own prior understanding of the terms and the sense given to the terms within the lecture.

### VARIATIONS

a Give out different terms to different trainees.
b Present the key terms embedded in a text about the subject.
c Make wall posters for display around the room before or after the lecture.
d Start by giving out the lecture topic and asking trainees to write down ten to twenty key words which they would expect to hear during the lecture. Write these words on transparencies or on a board or flipchart. You can add one or two key words of your own. You then use these words to guide your lecture. If you need time to plan your talk, collect the words the day/session before.

### RATIONALE/COMMENT

This process alerts trainees to key terms and encourages them to research them. As a result, trainees are likely to understand the talk better.

ACKNOWLEDGEMENTS/READING
I first learnt about using key words in lecture note-taking from Tony Buzan's *Use Your Head* (1974). Thanks to John Morgan for variation (c).

## SOCRATIC QUESTIONING

### Procedure

1 Form groups of eight or less.
2 Give each group a worksheet of carefully sequenced questions designed to guide participants to question assumptions or reach novel conclusions on old matters. (See the example sheet overleaf.)
3 As the group discussions develop, work with the groups to ensure that they are coming to the understanding you hoped for.

### VARIATIONS

a Trainees create their own question worksheets for peers on areas of personal interest or ones they have researched.
b Worksheets can contain open and closed questions as well as charts, figures and statements to complete.
c Design questions to stimulate open-ended enquiry to which you do *not* have particular answers in mind.

**2.8**

**MATERIALS**
A worksheet of questions

**TRAINEES**
Trainees with some experience who don't mind being led to a foregone conclusion!

**TRAINER**
Any

## RATIONALE/COMMENT

a Participant discoveries may be more meaningful and memorable than information received from the trainer.

b This process forces the trainer to work out logical steps for grasping points which they themselves learned a long time ago and may now consider easy or self-evident.

c An excellent activity for trainers who have the chance to work together.

READING

For variation (b), Britten (1985)

### Example worksheet

Students speaking in language classes

1 At what times and how often do you require your students to speak in your lessons?

2 What are all the things you do before, during and after the lesson if students/a student do(es) not speak?

3 Why do you think students don't speak?

4 Are there times in conversations when you don't speak? What's happening at those times?

5 At what age do children start talking in their own language? What are they doing during the earlier, 'silent' period?

6 How do you feel when you are silent in conversations? In group conversations?

7 How do you feel when your students are silent?

8 Why do you feel like this?

9 Do you think there may be a case for allowing language students 'a silent period'? When? For how long?

10 How would lessons, materials and so on need to be adapted to suit this idea of allowing a silent period?

© Longman Group UK Ltd 1992

## 2.9

**MATERIALS**
Questions, problems and tasks prepared for various stages of the lecture

**TRAINEES**
Any

# THE INTERACTIVE, OR INTERRUPTED LECTURE
## Procedure

1 Lecture for a few minutes and then stop.

2 Set trainees a question, problem or task in order to review content so far, check understanding of it or encourage prediction of future content. You can also probe trainees' personal experience (thus, 'Have you ever had this experience? What did you do about it? Did it work?'). Or you can work to reaffirm the confidence of the trainees. You can set problems that can only be solved by using information contained in the lecture so far. Tasks can be very simple. You can say, for example:

'Check with your neighbour . . .
- Can she spell that?
- Does she have the same number of points in section two as you do?
- Does she understand these points the same way as you do? If not, are there interesting differences?
- Does she feel that she will grasp this point after she has read about it and thought about it?
- Can she come up with two examples of this?
- Can she predict what might come next?
- Has she fallen asleep?
- Is she worried because she can't understand?'

**3** After your question/problem/test has been satisfactorily dealt with, move on.

#### RATIONALE/COMMENT

**a** This process allows you to rest between sections.
**b** Trainees are encouraged to speak and to think. This keeps them interested and awake.
**c** You can check comprehension of content so far before moving on.
**d** You need to think on your feet so that you can react to unpredictable points. This keeps *you* interested and awake.

ACKNOWLEDGEMENT
The first time I saw effective mid-lecture problem setting was in a lecture by Alan Cunningsworth.


# LISTEN, READ AND REST
## Procedure

**2.10**

**MATERIALS**
Several short reading passages that support, exemplify, summarise or expand on points made in the lecture

**TRAINEES**
Any

**1** Talk for five or ten minutes. Stop talking and hand out a passage that can be read in two or three minutes.
**2** Trainees read at their own pace, noting or marking anything they wish. Give enough time for everyone to finish the reading and then to rest for a moment. Don't speak at all during this time or during the reading phase.
**3** Trainees ask questions or make comments on the reading. When these have been dealt with, continue your lecture.

#### VARIATION
People can also write questions on the texts for each other or for you.

#### RATIONALE/COMMENT
This idea does not challenge the traditional 'one-way-flow-of-messages' assumption of the lecture process, but it does allow the audience to change modes occasionally. Reading can be done more at the trainees' own speed than listening can. This may reduce trainee fatigue and feel

freer. It is therefore vital that you do not talk at all while the participants are reading, resting and thinking.

ACKNOWLEDGEMENT
I learnt this from Mario Rinvolucri.

## 2.11

**MATERIALS**
A class set of notes for the lecture

**TRAINEES**
Any who have some experience of the content

# THE BACKWARDS LECTURE
## Preparation

Write out skeleton notes for the lecture, copy these and distribute them to all the trainees before the lecture.

## Procedure

1 In groups, trainees discuss your notes, fleshing them out and guessing at the arguments and detail. Make different groups responsible for different parts of the lecture.
2 Let each group choose someone to give their group's part of the lecture. It is up to the speakers to introduce, conclude, recap and make jokes, as a lecturer would. Those listening make additional notes if they wish to supplement the ones you have given them.
3 After each person has talked, anyone can ask for clarification. You can comment too.

**RATIONALE/COMMENT**
a All the trainees go home with a full set of notes.
b You can tell how much they have understood.
c Trainees hear lots of different voices.

ACKNOWLEDGEMENT
Roger Bowers gave me the name for this activity.

## 2.12

**MATERIALS**
A title for a talk; some background reading references

**TRAINEES**
Any

# PARTICIPANT MINI-LECTURES
## Preparation

In one session give several trainees a lecture title and some background reading or research references. They prepare mini-lectures on the topics you have given them, ready for the next session. You also need to tell them how long their talk should last.

## Procedure

1 In the next session the nominated trainees present their mini-lectures. After each talk you and other participants can ask questions or ask for clarification in the usual way.

2 During the presentations, you write down notes together with any queries, corrections and reading references.

3 Give copies of your notes to the trainees after the session. If you write neatly the first time and only have a few trainees, you can use a sheet of carbon paper under your note paper to make instant copies.

**VARIATIONS**

a Schedule either one or more than one mini-presentation per session.

b The mini-presentations can be on different themes or on the same theme from the same or different angles.

c Trainees choose their own topics.

**RATIONALE/COMMENT**

a This process encourages independent study. This may suit trainees who like doing private research.

b It allows lecturer and trainee to switch roles for a change. For example, trainees receive writing from you rather than the other way around.

c By switching roles everyone can gain insight into their new and their usual roles. When roles are switched back, there is usually more empathy on both sides.

# THE MIND-MAP LECTURE
## Procedure

**2.13**

**MATERIALS**
One or two large writing surfaces and pens or chalks

**TRAINEES**
Any

1 State the title of the talk and write it up in the centre of the board.

2 State the main areas to be covered in the talk and, while explaining these, draw main branches out from the central title on the board. Give each main branch a label to show the main area it represents. Write these labels in CAPITALS along the branches.

3 As you lecture, add branches and sub-branches to map further ideas and information onto the board. Thus, there is talk and visual support. (If the talk includes a lot of statistics or heavy detail, record these separately in note form on another board.)

4 As trainees ask questions or comment, add onto the mind map the extra points that arise.

5 Write up main ideas in one colour, side details in another and draw arrows and lines between points which are related. At the end of a lecture the board could look something like Figure 4 overleaf.

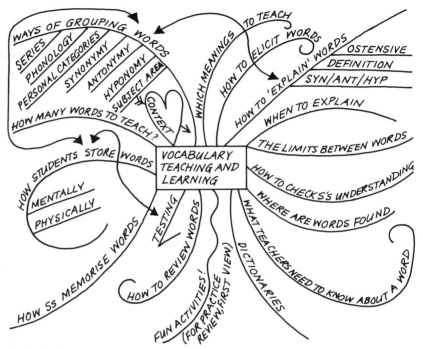

**Fig. 4** Mind map

**VARIATIONS**

**a** Draw your mind map(s) before the lecture to serve as prompts from which to speak.

**b** Trainees draw their own mind maps before or after a lecture to see how much they know or remember of the subject.

**c** Give out copies of a half-filled in mind map before a talk. Trainees fill it in as your talk progresses.

**d** Completing a half-filled in mind map can be a useful and challenging way of testing or reviewing previous lectures.

**e** A volunteer trainee stands at the board and draws a mind map for the lecture while you are talking. This way you get immediate visual feedback of what one trainee is understanding.

**f** As you get more practised at mind maps, you may like to include thin or thick lines, colour, shading, little diagrams, sharpness or fuzziness (on an OHP), two and three-dimensional drawing and other visual fun.

**RATIONALE/COMMENT**

**a** The mind map is non-linear and so does not force a particular sequence onto the lecturer. You can develop the mind map according to what comes up in the lecture and in the group and still retain organisation and overview.

**b** If you produce the mind map, trainees can see which areas you feel are most or least important as well as where their own questions and comments fit into the whole scheme of things.

c Mind maps are visually appealing, easy to rewrite or reorganise if too disorderly and they provide good support for non-native speakers who can thus gain the same message simultaneously in two different media.

d Mind maps are especially good for showing priorities as well as networks of connections between numbers of points.

e If some trainees dislike mind maps, feeling that they are spidery and disorganised, don't insist that they use them.

READING
Buzan (1974) and Woodward (1988e).

# INSTANT QUESTIONNAIRE FEEDBACK

## Procedure

1 After a lecture, ask the trainees to finish sentences such as the following:
*I could now list . . .*
*I feel good about . . .*
*I now know . . .*
*I don't understand . . .*
*I'd never thought of . . .*
*I can explain . . .*
*I'm really bored by . . .*
*I need practice at . . .*
*Do I really need to know . . . ?*
Choose sentence stems to suit the content of the lecture. You can either write them beforehand or during buzz-group time (see 2.5 *The buzz-group lecture*).

2 Once participants have finished the stems, ask them to read out their sentences to the whole class, discuss them in pairs, circulate them around the class, or hand them in (if they're written down).

### VARIATION

Instead of sentence stems, the questionnaire can contain whole statements which trainees respond to like this: 1 = Yes, 2 = Don't know/Not sure, 3 = No.

### RATIONALE/COMMENT

a The 'instant questionnaire' can be written fast and answered fast. It is thus a flexible means of getting instant feedback on a lecture.

b If you have time left at the end of the session, you can go over points that have caused trouble.

ACKNOWLEDGEMENT/READING
Gibbs (1981).

**2.14**

**MATERIALS**
A class set of sheets of paper with unfinished sentences on; or these can be dictated or listed on the board for trainees to copy

**TRAINEES**
Any

## 2.15

**MATERIALS**
None

**TRAINEES**
Any

# LECTURE EVALUATION FORM

## Procedure

1 Explain that you were never actually *taught* how to lecture, that you've just been doing it untrained and that you'd like to improve.
2 Hand out, either before, during or after the lecture, some sort of questionnaire. The example on page 35 is for use after a series of lectures has been given by the same person.
3 After you have made up a questionnaire, include some sort of scale, box or ticking system to the right of each item on it, for example:

| Definitely | Only somewhat | Not really | Not applicable |

4 Allow plenty of time for your audience to fill in the questionnaire anonymously and ask them to put the forms in a box on the way out.

### VARIATIONS

a Ask a colleague to observe you lecture, using either a specially made up questionnaire or any observation sheet that *you* use on trainees or teachers. Discuss the filled-in questionnaire with them afterwards.
b Issue trainees with coloured pieces of card. Ask them to show these when they are getting a bit lost. This is a non-verbal, unthreatening way for students to indicate they don't understand. Once a couple of cards have gone up, even really shy students will probably feel able to indicate incomprehension. Different colours can signify different kinds of problems, for example: Red = 'You're going too fast' Green = 'I don't understand'.
c You can use questionnaires to evaluate seminars and groupwork too.
d Participants evaluate their lectures overall on a scale from 5 to 1. First, they have to get together as a group and list the things they would expect from a lecturer before they awarded a particular grade.

### RATIONALE/COMMENT

a If trainees can see that their trainers are actively engaged in improving their own teaching, this can create a greater understanding of how teaching can continually be worked on and thought about.
b By gaining feedback and trying to change, you will be reminded of the difficulty of the process of accepting feedback, deciding to change and then actually effecting change. This can lead to more empathy with trainees.
c A course where everyone is trying to learn can breed a friendly, democratic atmosphere.

ACKNOWLEDGEMENTS/READING
I got the main idea here from an appendix in Bligh (1972). I learnt variation (d) from Herbert Puchta.

## Example questionnaire

### The lecturer

A *Maintains interest*
- Captures my interest at the start
- Varies the mode of presentation
- Indicates the start and end of major phases
- Stimulates activity in the audience
- Speaks audibly / has an appealing voice
- Uses aids effectively
- Looks at the audience
- Really likes the subject matter
- Links the lecture to other parts of the course
- Goes at the right pace for me
- Uses language in a way I like
  Comments: (Here the questionnaire should leave a few lines blank.)

B *Interprets the material*
- Offers her own ideas
- Offers other people's ideas
- Structures the material clearly
- Is clear and understandable as to minor points and qualifications
- Makes good use of relevant and interesting examples, illustrations and quotations
- Takes stock periodically
- Stresses important parts
- Makes it clear what the purpose of the lecture is
- Gives alternative explanations of difficult points
  Comments: (Again, blank lines here.)

C *Chooses material*
- Presents material appropriate to the needs and interests of the audience
- Organises material in an appropriate form for audience objectives
- Presents about the right amount of material each time
- Uses examples, verbal images and metaphors that are of special help to me

D *Makes clear what is expected of the audience*
- Clarifies, at the start, the value of note-taking
- Checks audience understanding and encourages feedback
- Makes clear what work might be advisable or necessary after the lecture

E *Other comments*
- Is there anything that the lecturer does that particularly distracts?
- Irritates?
- Pleases?
- Encourages?
- Discourages?
- Is there anything *specific* that you feel would improve the lecturer?

FURTHER READING FOR SECTION 1:
For good ideas on how to prepare and organise lecture material see *Improving Teaching in Higher Education* (UTMU 1976), for others on giving talks at conferences see Wright (1988). For general background see Bligh (1972), Bligh et al (1975), Beard and Hartley (1984), Brown (1978 and 1979), Buzan (1974), Evans (1988), Gibbs (1981), Gibbs et al (1984), Jones (no date), Lemke (1989), McLeish (1976), Poynton (1989), Rodgers (1986), Taylor (1988), and Verner and Dickinson (1968).

# Section 2: Input from the group

This section presents ways of drawing on the expertise in the group. It is not the trainer but the participants who play the central roles in introducing new ideas.

# THIRTY KILOS OF BOOKS
## Procedure

### SESSION 1

1 Bring in piles of EFL teachers' handbooks and resource books and put them in the middle of the room.
2 Give thirty-second to one-minute mini-reviews of as many of the books as you have time for.
3 Trainees take any book they like the look and sound of. Allow forty minutes for people to scan, dip in and swap. Let everyone take a book or two home to read and be prepared to talk about next session.

### SESSION 2

4 After reading at home, the trainees come back and tell each other about their books.

### VARIATIONS

a If you notice that a trainee has a special interest, guide her to relevant reading.
b Bring in books about cooking, martial arts, philosophy, maths . . . in fact, any subject *except* EFL. The trainees' task is to find interesting parts in the reading which parallel their own EFL work. At the next meeting people make presentations (in small groups) on what they read and how they feel it is relevant to their own work or to EFL in general.

### RATIONALE/COMMENT

a Books recommended face to face are often read with greater interest than those on a book list.
b You can save trainees a lot of time by selecting reading that is especially appropriate for them.
c Seeing what someone picks to share with the group is interesting in itself.
d The input comes from many sources and comes into the group via the minds and personalities of the participants.

ACKNOWLEDGEMENTS
I learnt the main idea from Mario Rinvolucri and variation (b) from John Morgan and Gerry Kenny.

## 2.16

**MATERIALS**
About thirty kilos of books which you know well enough to be able to summarise orally in a few sentences each

**TRAINEES**
Especially good for those who like reading but are away from home and from their own books

**SESSIONS**
Two

**TIME IN THE COURSE**
Especially good if Session 1 is just before a weekend or a holiday and Session 2 just after

# STARTER QUESTION CIRCLE
## Procedure

1 Everyone sits in a circle.
2 Either you or one of the trainees introduces a topic – for example, 'starting lessons' – in the form of a question such as, 'What do you do when you first go into a classroom?'

## 2.17

**MATERIALS**
None

**TRAINEES**
Trainees with classroom experience

3  Each person in the circle gives *one* answer to the question, that is, one thing they do when they first go into a class. For example, Trainee A might say, 'I ask the students how they are'.

4  Other people in the circle are allowed to ask *factual* questions only. For example: 'Do you ask them in the mother tongue or in the target language?' 'Do you ask people by name or just throw the question out to the group?' 'Have you taught different responses to your question in earlier classes?'

5  Trainee A answers the questions one by one, as they are asked, again giving only factual information. The other trainees are not allowed to make statements such as, 'Oh, I do that too' or 'I do that but I . . .' or to make judgmental comments such as 'But then they just sit and stare at you!' This is a strict rule and has to be mentioned at the start.

6  Once Trainee A has answered all the factual questions, the next trainee says what they normally do when they first go into a classroom, and then answers any factual questions in the same way. The question continues to travel around the circle.

7  Arrange things so that your turn is towards the end. If time and ideas allow, the question can travel around the group twice.

**VARIATIONS**

a  A big class can divide into several smaller groups. Group secretaries record ideas for later discussion in plenary.

b  The starter question can be chosen to *pre*view or *re*view areas of interest.

c  Trainees can use this process without you being present. If they keep a record and give you a copy, you can move on from these ideas in the following session.

**RATIONALE/COMMENT**

a  As people listen to each other without expressing judgments and without pulling rank, ideas can emerge without being shot down instantly.

b  Ideas come from everyone.

c  People get a peep into each other's classrooms without actually going in to observe.

d  You get insights into the present state of practice within the group and so you can slip in ideas towards the end that fit in with or start from your group's present practice.

e  *Concrete* details of teaching are heard and discussed by working professionals.

ACKNOWLEDGEMENT/READING
Teachers at The British Schools Day in Brindisi evolved this technique for me when I worked with them as a visiting trainer in 1986. See Woodward (1987e and 1988b).

# PULLING STRINGS, OR INDIRECT INPUT

## Procedure

**2.18**

**MATERIALS**
None

**TRAINEES**
Any

1 Describe a technique or activity to one trainee privately before a session. The trainee asks as many questions as necessary to get the feel of the new technique. An example technique could be: keeping part of the board free to accommodate new vocabulary that comes up in a lesson.
2 In the next group session the trainee presents this technique to the group.
3 Afterwards, the presenter, the other trainees and you discuss the idea together.

### RATIONALE/COMMENT

In this process of mediated trainer input you have a chance to be in the group and to watch a trainee presenting an idea. Presenters have a chance to try an idea out with the group before trying it out with their own classes.

# CREATIVE WORKSHOPS

## Procedure

**2.19**

**MATERIALS**
A framework or set of principles to apply to a content area

**TRAINEES**
Any

1 Introduce a particular framework or set of guiding principles by explanation, demonstration or experiential process (see example overleaf.)
2 'Hand over' this framework or set of principles to the trainees. They discuss it in groups and test it out.
3 After the individual or group work there is whole group discussion of whether or how the principles or framework can be applied and of any adaptations or new ideas thought up.

### NOTE

Everyone has been discussing/using the same framework but different groups generally come up with different adaptations and ideas within this framework. These adaptations and ideas constitute new input for the group.

*Example framework: Component questions (broadening known activities or concepts)*

1 Take a traditional idea

Take a teaching activity that you feel you know well, preferably a traditional one, for example, dictation.

2 Ask very basic questions.

Break down the activity, mentally, and ask as many simple questions about the activity as you can. Questions about dictation might be:

| | |
|---|---|
| Who reads? | What is the text? |
| Do they read aloud? | Where is the text? |
| How fast do they read? | Is the text words or something |
| What sort of voice do they read in? | else? |
| When do they pause? | Who listens? |
| Who do they read to? | Who writes? Where do they write? |
| What do they do while they read? | What do they write with? |
| Where do they read from? | What else could the listener do apart from write words? |

And so on. You'll need at least fifteen questions.

3 Create zany answers

Take one of your questions, for example, from above, 'How fast do they read?' and create an unusual answer such as 'As fast as they possibly can'.

4 Create good reasons for doing the zany idea

Now think about what would happen if this actually took place in a classroom. Obviously, the students wouldn't be able to get the dictation down.

Now, to come up with some interesting solutions, you need to find answers to questions like, 'Why would this be a good idea?' or 'What would have to happen next?' Or, in this case, 'What would the students have to do to get the dictation down?' They would have to ask the teacher to stop and repeat and spell things and give punctuation, and so on.

What language would this practise? Requests, such as 'Could you say that again, please?', 'How do you spell that?', 'What does that word mean?', 'What comes next?', 'OK, go on!' This is very useful language which students will need in conversation in English.

5 You can apply this 'Component questions' technique to *any* teaching activity, e.g. 'setting up groupwork', 'playing a tape', 'reading a short story' and 'taking the register'. When you've come up with your new ideas, check the magazines and handbooks to see if anyone has published them yet.

© Longman Group UK Ltd 1992

## VARIATIONS

**a** Simpler, shorter frameworks can be used too, for example, 'minimal reconstruction' in correcting students' written work. The basic idea here is that when correcting written work, you think of all the ways you could correct a given sentence or phrase and then you choose the one that alters the student's version least. The principle can be demonstrated in plenary by using an incorrect sentence from a piece of student writing. Once the sentence and the corrections have been discussed and the least disrupting correction chosen, trainees move into groups to discuss and correct more student work.

**b** Other simple frameworks that can be used as the basis of creative workshops are:

- 'reformulation' of student utterances (Wilberg 1987),
- the application of a receptive skills model to lesson planning with textbook listening material (Harmer 1983, pp. 142–99),
- headings for workable lesson plans (see 5.1 *Basic lesson plans*).

### RATIONALE/COMMENT

Merely handing out good ideas, frameworks or sets of principles to trainees does not guarantee that they will be understood, used or transferred to new situations. The creative workshop process allows time for people to discuss and test out given input. This will lead to discussion of the problems of application and the adjustments necessary. Not only does this encourage trainees to question input and test its relevance, but it also forces trainers to recognise that some ideas travel well and others don't.

ACKNOWLEDGEMENT/READING
The example framework originally appeared in Woodward (1989e).

# DISCOVERY WORK

## Procedure

1 Give trainees a useful, interesting and motivating task to do either in your session, in their own language classrooms or elsewhere (see the examples below). Trainees work individually, in pairs or in small groups.
2 Make sure that each group has the resources it needs and that everyone understands the task. After that, act only as a resource person or catalyst for individuals or groups that are stuck.
3 The individuals and/or groups work towards an outcome of *their* choosing.
4 Trainees share these outcomes in plenary.
5 From the discussion of particular tasks and outcomes, you and the group draw out more general principles.

**2.20**

**MATERIALS**
Enough tasks and resources for each group

**TRAINEES**
Good for trainees who like to work away from the trainer, alone or with others

Example discovery tasks

*A Language discovery task*

Listen out in real life for the word *actually* when it is used in conversation. Note down, *verbatim*, instances of its occurrences (with context). From these instances, what meanings and functions does the word seem to have?
(From Gerry Kenny and Bonnie Tsai)

*B Lesson planning discovery task*

Ask people in the group what kind of planning they do in their lives . . . for the future (pensions, holidays), against accidents (crash helmets, insurance), for daily activities (memos, lists), for creations (cakes, reports, paintings), or for other reasons. Ask people why they plan, how they plan, what they do with the plans, whether the planning is helpful or effective, if they ever alter their plans, when and why. What do these discussions lead you to think about planning for lessons and courses?
(Kenny and Tsai inspired)

*C Language research discovery task*

Consider the following sentences:

There are some apples. | Are there any pears left?
They haven't got any magazines. | Would you like some tea?

What language point is at issue? What answer would you give to a language student who questioned you on this issue? Check this advice with colleagues and with the grammar books provided.
Now consider these sentences:
I like some pop music.
I like any pop music.
I don't like some pop music.
(Lewis and Hill 1985)

**VARIATIONS**

**a** Each group can have the same or different tasks.

**b** Present a choice of tasks, with trainees choosing the most relevant to them.

**c** Give one large task to a plenary group. Everyone discusses how to divide the task and the labour.

**d** Trainees suggest their own tasks. Their ideas may spring from reading, from language students' queries or their own teaching practice.

**e** Trainees present outcomes in poster form.

**f** Each group gets a widthways strip of an OHP transparency. They write their main finding on it (with OHP pens). In plenary all the strips are put onto the OHP, displayed and discussed.

**g** If all the individuals or groups are working in the same room on the same or similar tasks, each group appoints a 'runner' whose job it is to go to the other groups, see how they are working and give out information on the way the runner's own group is progressing. This can unstick groups without you having to intervene – that is, unless *all* the groups are stuck! (If this happens, there is probably something wrong with the task or the task instructions.)

**RATIONALE/COMMENT**

**a** Participants are actively involved. They can have practice, with others, in working through useful real-life tasks which they must undertake, often alone, in their teaching lives.

**b** It is possible that you may see one outcome as the best, but this goes against the open-ended 'discovery' feeling of this process and can cause intense frustration and demotivation in the groups.

**c** *Real* discovery, with its 'Eureka!' or 'Ah ha!' feeling, can make things especially satisfying and memorable.

ACKNOWLEDGEMENT/READING
I learnt variation (f) from Rod Bolitho. See also Britten (1985) and UTMU (1976).

# GUIDED FANTASY

## Procedure

**2.21**

**MATERIALS**
Any

**TRAINEES**
Any

**1** When trainees are relaxed and comfortable, give them a term which they have said they would like to investigate together, for example: 'learner independence', 'teacher development', or 'action research'.

**2** Next, ask trainees to close their eyes. You then lead them through a visualisation of the term. As you talk, they experience the ideas and images that come up in association with your words.

For example, if the term chosen is 'learner independence', ask trainees to imagine that they will see and hear the perfect environment for learner independence. They enter an ideal school for this and go around looking at the rooms and resources, sampling the atmosphere and meeting the staff and students. After each element – for example, 'rooms' – allow time for trainees to imagine the rooms and to mentally note the things they experience during their imaginary journey around this perfect environment.

**3** After a few minutes, gently ask people to 'come back' to the training room and open their eyes when they are ready.

**4** Next, trainees share their experiences. Ask them to recall all the ideas, sights and sounds they experienced. Next they discuss how they could make their imagined environment a real one.

**RATIONALE/COMMENT**
This process can come before trainer input as preparation or, depending on how much comes up, can replace trainer input altogether.

ACKNOWLEDGEMENT/READING
I learnt this from Herbert Puchta. See Lindstromberg (1990 p. 88) for an example of visualisation applied to language teaching.

## 2.22

**MATERIALS**
Written transcripts
of the thoughts and
opinions of people
outside the group

**TRAINEES**
Any

# VOICES FROM OUTSIDE THE GROUP

## Preparation

Trainees can be given or asked to find transcripts from interviews or lessons, sections from learner diaries or student feedback sheets, or other written sources of peoples' thoughts and opinions. They will need to assure the writers' anonymity or else gain permission.

## Procedure

Each trainee reads their material out to the group as if they were the author. For example, if learner diaries have been kept by learners on a language course, extracts can be typed up, with the learners' permission. During a discussion in a teacher training session, participants in the discussion can read aloud relevant extracts as if they were the language students concerned.

### RATIONALE/COMMENT

This process brings in a new variety of voices and points of view from outside the group. It can be especially useful if the training group is very small or has been together for a long time and become rather jaded with each other. Outside voices can come in at the start or during a session, or can round off a session, thus giving language learners the last word.

## 2.23

**MATERIALS**
Pens and paper for
everyone

**TRAINEES**
Any

# GHOSTS BEHIND THE BOARD

## Procedure

1 Ask your trainees to think back over the total number of teachers they've had in their lifetimes, whether in primary or secondary schools, at university, or for a hobby or part-time interest. Compare the numbers.

2 Now, ask everyone to think back to a good learning memory – a time when they were with a teacher and felt very good. Ask them to remember as much as possible about the time, place and circumstances, and to write this down in a paragraph.

3 Next, trainees get into groups of about five and share anything they would like to about their memories.

4 After this, in plenary, invite participants to relate any particularly interesting memory told by someone else in their group.

5 Next, ask everyone to think back to a 'bad ghost', to an unpleasant encounter with a teacher – and, again, they try to remember as much detail as possible and then write a few lines about it.

### EXTENSION

Once participants have recalled and 'established' their own good and bad ghosts, these can be referred to by the trainees or by the trainer throughout the rest of the course. Thus, any subject, such as teacher voice and dress, gesture, use of board and book, discipline and praise can be discussed with reference to the ghosts. For example, 'How would your good ghost, Miss X, handle this, do you think?' or, after an observation, 'That sounds like something my bad ghost, Mr Y, would have said/done.'

### RATIONALE/COMMENT
Anybody who has been to school has views on what a good or bad teacher is. They have watched teachers at work, even if absent-mindedly, for thousands of hours. This is a kind of work experience – from the other side of the desk.

These memories, especially good and bad ghosts, often profoundly affect their beliefs about teaching and learning. It is as well to get these memories out in the open early on in a course so that consolidation, unlearning or relearning can begin before more input is crammed in on top of old.

### ACKNOWLEDGEMENT/READING
This guided recall option is just one idea from the work of Ephraim Weintraub on 'teacher residual memories'. It was at a workshop of Ephraim's, at the 1988 IATEFL Conference, that I finally experienced this activity led by its originator after encountering it, through others, for years before. See Weintraub (1989).

# Section 3: Experiential learning

This section may appeal to people who say, 'Let's stop talking about it. Let's do it!' It capitalises on the parallels between language classrooms and training rooms, and involves the following assumptions:
- Trainers need to practise what they preach.
- Participants can learn by doing.
- Training can be demystified.
- Participants can learn about content *and* process at the same time.
- Almost any experience in a training session can be a source of insight. For confusion to be avoided, it is vital that you routinely and explicitly signal the role changes you ask trainees to undergo during experiential phases (e.g. from participant as trainee teacher to participant as language learner). Also, trainees need time and, possibly, help after an experiential process experience to analyse it, reflect on it and come back to themselves.

## 2.24

**MATERIALS**
Depends on the exercise; see below

**TRAINEES**
Good for physically active or restless trainees

# BORROWING A LANGUAGE CLASSROOM EXERCISE

## Preparation

Decide on a language classroom activity that you would like to teach to trainees. Prepare any material trainees will need to do the activity.

## Procedure

1 Suggest that trainees actually experience an activity rather than just read about it, listen to it or talk about it.
2 Ask them to pretend they are language students. Do the activity with them, in English, with yourself in the role of the language teacher.
3 Afterwards, encourage trainees to comment on what they did in the activity, on the advantages and disadvantages the activity might have in a language classroom, and on how they felt when doing it.
4 Allow time for trainees to note down the steps of the activity and any other information they wish.

**VARIATIONS**

a With native-speaker trainees, do the activity in a foreign language so they can experience, in more respects, what a language student might feel.
b Trainees do the activity in their mother tongue but change the content of the activity so that it is more useful to them. For example, a 'Find someone who . . .' activity could be done with Italian trainees in Italian, but could include sentences such as 'Find someone who knows what behaviourism is'.

**RATIONALE/COMMENT**

a Doing the activity in the mother tongue means that trainees only learn about the *activity*. Doing it in a foreign language they are not fluent in not only helps them to learn some language but also gives insight on what it feels like to work in a foreign language.
b Participants may remember activities better because they have done them.
c Discussion of an activity, after it has been experienced, is generally lively and relevant.
d Encourage trainees to notice the language the teacher needs to set the activity up as well as the language they need to negotiate with each other and carry out the activity.

ACKNOWLEDGEMENT/READING
The first person I ever met who said, in an EFL teacher training session, 'Let's not *talk* about it, let's *do* it', was Ruth Kasarda.

See Woodward (1988a and 1991). For variation (a) see Golebiowska (1985) and for (b) see Aiello *et al* (1987).

# OPEN PROCESS, OR DISCUSSING PROCESS DECISIONS

## Procedure

**MATERIALS**
None

**TRAINEES**
Good for trainees
who always want
to know 'why'

As you move through the session, comment on the constraints you see operating, your range of choices and the rationale for your decisions. Thus, you might say, 'I've run out of material now, so I could send you home early at this point. I do, however, have some "fillers" in my repertoire. One seems to fit in quite well with the theme of this session, so I think we'll do that.' Or, again, 'I don't think I'll read you another long quote. You've had quite a lot of them.'

### VARIATIONS

a Open process commentary can be retrospective, for example, 'Last night I was thinking that we hadn't really done enough on the *reasons* for structuring writing lessons the way I suggested. So today we're going to . . .'

b You can use this process after a session is over when you and the trainees are sitting around having a cup of tea together.

c You can lay options for activities before the group and they can decide what to do in the circumstances, for example, 'Do you like having OHPs read to you or would you rather read them yourselves?'

d You can give advanced notice of process changes. For instance, 'OK. Some more reading aloud coming up.'

### RATIONALE/COMMENT

a This helps demystify the training process.

b Participants can gain information on real-life classroom decision-making (yours), and apply it in their own classrooms if they wish.

c You are encouraged to be clear about your own principles, motives and practice.

READING
Brumfit (1979) and Goffman (1971).

# RECORDING PROCESS CHOICES

## Procedure

**MATERIALS**
A form for each
participant (see
Step 2)

**TRAINEES**
Any

**CONTENT**
Good for studying
classroom
management

1 During the session, use a variety of techniques relating to the session topic. For example, if your session is on classroom management, use different ways of starting and stopping groupwork, checking tasks, attracting attention and so on.

2 Towards the end of the session, hand out a form which has headings such as 'Note down one way in which people were split into pairs' or 'Note down two ways in which group tasks were checked'. Thinking back over the session so far, participants fill in the form. That is, they make 'process' or 'how' notes, not 'content' or 'what' notes.

**3** Participants can keep this record sheet to build up a store of classroom management ideas in their files.

### VARIATIONS

**a** You can give out the whole form before the session or, alternatively, introduce each heading over a number of sessions. The first heading can relate to the start of a session, for example, 'How was the session started?' Next time, keep the earlier heading and add a new one.

**b** The first time or two, talk trainees through the form, filling it in as you go. In later sessions, they fill it in themselves in pairs or groups with you on hand to help. Later still, individual participants or groups fill it in on their own.

**c** Participants change the headings and the design of the form to suit their interests.

### RATIONALE/COMMENT

**a** This process encourages recall of all parts of a session, an interest in process as well as content, orderliness in note-taking and good variety in, for example, classroom management techniques.

**b** Learning happens through experience, which is followed up by explicit commentary.

ACKNOWLEDGEMENT/READING
Patricia Mugglestone started me off in this area. See Mugglestone (1979) and Woodward (1991).

## 2.27

**MATERIALS**
Depends on the content of the session

**TRAINEES**
Especially useful for trainees who have a low tolerance for listening to lectures and who like to learn by doing and thinking simultaneously

# LOOP INPUT

## Procedure

**1** Choose a process for the session that exactly matches the content. For example, let us suppose that your content is 'The advantages and disadvantages of using role plays in language teaching; how to give out roles, help people into role, building the atmosphere for a role play; and how to start, monitor, stop and give feedback on a role play'. Your process can be, for example, as follows:

**a** Divide trainees into two groups.

**b** Group A brainstorms the advantages, Group B the disadvantages of using role plays.

**c** Set the scene of a staffroom during the coffee break. One person from Group A acts the part of a pro-role play teacher while a person from Group B acts the part of an anti-role play teacher. They meet in the staffroom and discuss the pros and cons of role plays.

**d** While the role play is taking place, you can stroll around and unobtrusively note down examples of people acting well in role. After the role play, give your feedback to the group, commenting on interesting exchanges or good use of persuasive tactics.

**2** Ask trainees to recall the *steps* of the session so far.

**3** Now go deeper into the *content* of the session. That is, for the example above, you might ask the trainees to report the way you gave out roles, helped people into role, set the scene, started the role play off, what you noted down, how you stopped the role play and gave feedback on it.

**4** Elicit other ways that role plays can be set up, monitored, followed on from and so forth, so that trainees are not left with the message that the way it was done here is the only 'right' way.

Note:.During the first stage of the session, the participants experience the content of the session through experiencing its process.

### RATIONALE/COMMENT

**a** Trainees experience activities by doing them.

**b** Although trainees experience activities, they are not, as is sometimes the case in experiential training, asked to take on a role that is very different from their actual role on the course. They are allowed to stay as trainees or teachers.

**c** An activity frame is borrowed from the language classroom and brought into the training room but is used directly for the purpose of the trainee's *own* syllabus. The consistency between the process of training and your message is thus total.

READING
Woodward (1991).

# PROCESS TICKS

## Preparation

**1** Prepare a list of all the steps you plan to take in a particular session, or part of a session. Then include more steps, ones that are possible but which you do not actually plan to take.

**2** Duplicate a class set.

## Procedure

**1** Hand out the list at the beginning of the session.

**2** Ask trainees to tick off, on the list, the steps that you actually take as they notice you taking them. As you go through the session you may well miss out some of the steps on your list and add others that you did not put on it.

**3** Ask the trainees to discuss what steps you took. Point out any discrepancies between planned and actual steps. Trainees can ask why you made certain changes or what other steps would have been possible.

**2.28**

**MATERIALS**
A class set of a list of process steps relevant to your session

**TRAINEES**
Any

**RATIONALE/COMMENT**

**a** This process encourages you and trainees to pay attention to process as well as content, both in sessions and in planning.

**b** It shows that it's OK to depart from a plan.

ACKNOWLEDGEMENT

I got the germ of this idea at IATEFL, Edinburgh 1988 from an ESP session run by David Wilson of Specialist Language Services, York.

## 2.29

**MATERIALS**
Enough teaching ideas/recipes for each participant

**TRAINEES**
Good for trainees who know each other somewhat

**NUMBER OF SESSIONS**
Usually more than one

# GIFT-GIVING, OR THE CHANGING ROOM

## Procedure

1 For each of your trainees, choose a teaching activity that you feel they will like or that will suit them. Present each activity, orally or on paper, to each trainee. Do this apart from the group. The trainee may, of course, ask questions.

2 After the necessary preparation time, the trainee demonstrates the activity to the group, who join in and do it.

3 The trainee and the group discuss the steps of the activity, its advantages and disadvantages and their feelings when doing it. They can also discuss whether the choice of gift activity was apt.

**VARIATIONS**

**a** Give each trainee a choice of activities to do.

**b** Explain the activity by showing a video of it being done, or arrange for some other teacher or trainer to explain it.

**c** Give activities to only one or some of the participants.

**d** Trainees 'give' activities to each other.

**e** In any one session, one or more participants present their activities.

**RATIONALE/COMMENT**

**a** Trainees have a chance to be the teacher/trainer.

**b** They have a chance to try out activities they might later like to use in their classrooms.

**c** They can learn from each other.

**d** The way you get across the idea to the trainee will sometimes be quite different from the way the trainee gets the idea across to the group. This way *you* can learn something too.

**e** Discussing the way activities have mutated can be interesting and, in the long run, may encourage creativity.

**f** The choice of gift says much about both giver and receiver.

ACKNOWLEDGEMENT

I first learnt this from John Morgan.

# CHAPTER 3

# *Reactions to information*

The overall aim of this chapter is to provide ways for trainees to get interested in information by reacting to it. The ideas here help trainees to be active and the material to be absorbed or 'owned' in some way. (I have not covered live teaching in this section. That is in Chapter 5, *The teaching encounter*.)

Drawing on Davis (1979), we can class sources of information about teaching as follows:

The written word
Whole books, selected chapters and extracts, articles, handouts, lesson plans, lists and random arrays, essays, charts, diagrams, teachers' books, coursebooks, EFL tests and exercises, lesson transcripts, examiners' reports, language samples for study, practice books, grammar books, diaries, case studies, teachers' magazines.

The spoken word
Coursebook and teacher-produced tapes of texts, dialogues, drills and songs; samples of native and non-native language on tape; taped lessons and lectures; samples of pronunciation features; films and TV programmes; interviews with native and non-native speakers, 'experts' and professional people.

Pictures
Published teaching resources such as wallcharts, flashcards, picture stories, games and cartoons, as well as teacher-made magazine picture libraries and so on.

Activities in this chapter are divided up into three sections: 'Mostly before', 'Mostly during' and 'Mostly after', that is, before, during or after interaction with any of the sources of information listed above. This three-way division echoes the popular 'pre-skills', 'in-skills' and 'post-skills' model of classroom EFL work with the receptive skills. Many of the activities within the sections will be familiar to the trained EFL teacher. Here they are applied to information sources appropriate to the teacher-training classroom. Again, as with all the processes presented in this book, it is possible that once trainees have experienced these ways of working in the *training* classroom, they may choose to adapt them for use in their own language classrooms.

## Section 1: Mostly before

**3.1**

**MATERIALS**
None

**TRAINEES**
Any

# MAPPING WHAT YOU ALREADY KNOW
## Procedure

1 Tell trainees the subject matter of the session. Before introducing the information, ask them to think for a few minutes about what they know of the subject already.

2 Ask them to write down in notes, lists, brainstorm arrays or mind maps the thoughts that occur to them. Thus, if you are about to do some work on listening comprehension, a trainee might come up with a mind map like Figure 5 before you start. Or they might come up with something completely different!

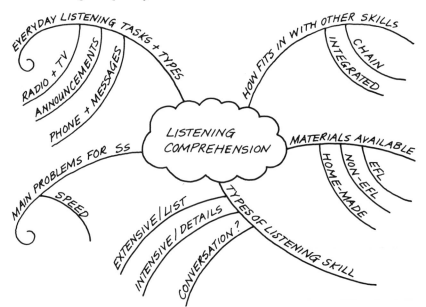

**Fig. 5** Mind map on listening comprehension

**3** Trainees show each other and/or you their notes and talk through the similarities and differences between them.

**4** As trainees work with the information, or after they've finished, they can go back to their notes to fill them out.

**5** (Optional) Present further input, perhaps by using one of the processes in Chapter 2.

### EXTENSION

**6** If trainees show you their maps, you can make sure you move on from what they know rather than causing frustration by teaching it again!

### VARIATIONS

**a** Trainees can use this technique when studying alone before a session. They bring their 'maps' to the session, ready to compare them with other people's.

**b** Mapping what you don't know is equally useful.

### RATIONALE/COMMENT

**a** In the main idea, trainees have a chance to review and recall what they know already, before being bombarded with new information.

**b** Through the sharing of 'maps' there is group recall and learning.

**c** Mapping new information onto old makes new learning visible. People can see how much they've learned and how it integrates with what they already know.

# DIVIDING UP TASKS

## Procedure

**3.2**

**MATERIALS**
Class set of information sources (see Step 1); handouts of task descriptions

**TRAINEES**
Any

**1** Give trainees the information together with all the instructions for a large task. For example:

    **a** a reading list and a reading assignment,

    **b** a video on language learning and a task sheet,

    **c** a sound tape of some non-native speakers and instructions to note pronunciation errors.

You need enough copies of the information and task for all the trainees.

**2** Once the trainees have managed to grasp what is entailed in the task – and this may include plenty of discussion, listing of steps and questioning – they decide how they will break up the task between them.

**3** Ask them to produce:

    **a** a list of who is doing which part of the task,

    **b** a path or procedure for the task,

    **c** a timescale for each person and for each part of the task.

**4** Each member of the group gets copies of what they agreed in Step 3.

**RATIONALE/COMMENT**

**a** By meeting a large task as a group, planning work on it together and dividing the labour, the task can seem less daunting and the group is able to set its own timescales independently of the trainer.

**b** By listening to the preliminary, organisational discussion and answering questions, you can spot any confusions or dead ends before people get into the task.

## 3.3

**MATERIALS**
An information source, e.g. a book or article (see Step 1)

**TRAINEES**
Any

# PREDICTING WHAT COMES NEXT

## Procedure

**1** Show the trainees a tiny part of the information source (e.g. of a book or article, the first paragraph or the first and last lines of a paragraph; of a film, the first few frames; of a lesson plan, the pictures or diagrams accompanying it or its statement of aim; of a taped dialogue, the first utterance . . . ).

**2** Ask trainees to predict something from this first glimpse. The 'something' could be the professional terminology that they expect to come up in an article, the sequence of activities that might be used in a lesson, the nationality of a speaker, the rest of a sentence, or the continuation of a conversational exchange. Ask trainees to note down their predictions.

**3** Expose more of the information and allow trainees to compare their predictions with what actually comes up in it. For example, if the trainees predicted that the form *Would you like to . . . ?* was likely to come up in a conversation based on role-play cards during a lesson on invitations, they can compare this with the *Fancy coming?* and *Like to . . . ?* that were actually used.

**4** Discussion is based on the differences between predictions and reality.

**VARIATION**

Once trainees know this idea they can use it when studying alone at home.

**RATIONALE/COMMENT**

**a** Trainees have a chance to tune into the subject of an information source and get their preconceptions, thoughts and prejudices out into the open. They can then compare these with what actually turns up in the information. This will help them to stay awake and active.

**b** Later discussion is likely to be lively if there are big differences between predictions and reality.

**c** Predicting what language will come up in an activity and then comparing this with what people actually say can give surprising results.

# Section 2: Mostly during

## IN-QUESTIONS

### Preparation

1 Mentally or physically divide the information source (such as a reading text) up into sections.
2 Work out what you expect trainees to learn from each section.
3 Design questions to check this learning.
4 If your information source is a text, cut it up into sections, and paste the sections onto a sheet of paper with the checking questions written between the sections. Because these questions are interspersed within the text, I call them 'in-questions'.

### Procedure

Ask trainees to proceed through the work using the information source and reacting to the in-questions alternately. They can work on the in-questions individually or together.

#### VARIATIONS

a Different trainees study different sections of the information source and write in-questions for each other. Everyone then studies all the information with all the trainee-made in-questions attached.
b Trainees who are able to come to a session and work with the information prepare in-questions to help trainees who could not attend.
c Provide in-questions for trainees working on information individually.
d Break up lectures with oral in-questions (and with swift bits of recapping too).
e OHPs can be used too. Reveal the first section and mask the second. Either write your in-questions onto your transparency or have them near you so that you can ask them and discuss the answers before revealing the next section.
f If your information source is a sound or video tape, in-questions can be recorded onto the tape, be asked by the trainer using the pause button, or be written on a handout.

#### RATIONALE/COMMENT

a Breaking the information up into sections, and preparing and answering in-questions all foster a good understanding of the material.
b Answering in-questions between sections checks comprehension before moving on to new information. With some types of material this is necessary, since without thoroughly understanding the basics very little can be gained from working with later related subject matter.

## 3.4

**MATERIALS**
Scissors, paper, pen and a copying method for texts or a cassette player or video with a pause button

**TRAINEES**
Any

**CONTENT**
Any, but especially content where understanding of later parts depends on clear understanding of earlier parts

## 3.5

MATERIAL
Tippex, or white-
out; copies of a
gapped text and of
the original,
ungapped version

TRAINEES
Any

# FILLING IN GAPS

## Preparation

1 Take a text and work out which words you would like to make disappear. Depending on the kind of text it is, you might choose to 'white out':
   - professional terms or their definitions,
   - the names of models (e.g. of different lesson structures) or of theories (e.g. of language acquisition),
   - the names of stages of activities that are described,
   - parts of a dialogue between a student and a teacher bent on error correction,
   - the names of tenses,
   - exponents of a function,
   - concept questions from the transcript of the presentation stage of a lesson on a particular language point.
2 Either white words out or recreate the information source without them in. Make copies for trainees.

## Procedure

1 Trainees read the information a couple of times to get the overall idea. Then they work individually or together to fill in the gaps.
2 They check against a correctly filled-in version of the original information source, for example, in a book or on OHP.

### VARIATIONS

a Texts can be gapped differently so that trainees dictate the gap fillings to each other.
b All the trainees have different texts from each other.
c Trainees work on gapped texts alone at home.

### RATIONALE/COMMENT

Instead of casting a glazed eye across a full page of text, trainees have to stop, think, commit themselves and check – that is, they have to interact with the data. Hopefully, this will stimulate interest, understanding and recall.

# TRANSFERRING INFORMATION FROM ONE FORMAT TO ANOTHER

**3.6**

**MATERIALS**
An information source

**TRAINEES**
Any

## Preparation

Look at your information source to see what sort of information it contains and how this information could be presented in a different form. In Figure 6, information contained in the left-hand column could be represented as suggested in the right-hand column.

| | |
|---|---|
| a) a lesson plan | ⟶ seating diagrams |
| b) a text | ⟶ two columns headed 'Advantages' and 'Disadvantages' |
| c) a tape of a non-native speaker | ⟶ notation of stress errors |
| d) a talk about teaching | ⟶ a recipe for a language-learning activity |
| e) a TV programme | ⟶ notes of what people liked or disliked, understood or couldn't understand |
| f) a case study | ⟶ some ideas for self-access work |
| g) a teacher's resource book | ⟶ a mind map of the main ideas |
| h) a tape of a lesson | ⟶ a lesson transcript |
| i) other people's essays | ⟶ adaptations to one's own essay |
| j) wallcharts | ⟶ language they could be used to practise |
| k) a song or dialogue | ⟶ a lesson plan for its exploitation |

**Fig. 6** Transferring information: variations

## Procedure

Set the task of transferring information from the original source into an appropriate (different) format. Trainees can do the task in class or at home.

### RATIONALE/COMMENT

This process involves understanding information well enough to be able to represent it in a different form. This probably means that the information is processed more thoroughly and by different brain cells! It certainly requires flexibility and is more challenging and less boring than simple regurgitation or passive reading or listening.

## 3.7

**MATERIALS**
A 'maze' (see
Figure 7)

**TRAINEES**
Any

# MAZE DISCUSSIONS

## Preparation

1 Choose a particular area that trainees would enjoy/benefit from discussing. Mazes can be about personal and professional dilemmas, options that open up to a teacher as she goes through a lesson, curriculum and planning choices, error analysis and correction choices or any other matter that involves dilemmas and choices (most of life in fact!).
2 Write out the situation and the steps of its development on an ordered series of cards (see Figure 7). The top card describes the entry situation, which includes a dilemma of some kind. Immediately below the description of this situation, on the same card, are brief descriptions of two or more options for possible action.
3 Index each option with the number of a card further into the stack.
4 These later cards bear descriptions of the (often problematic) consequences of the option which led to that card, along with further numbered options leading to further cards. Some later cards describe an ending to the situation. These latter cards are 'exit' cards.

## Procedure

1 One trainee or group of trainees reads the top card(s) and describes the entry situation to the other group members.
2 The reader(s) then proceed to read the first set of options.
3 The group discusses the options and chooses one. The one they choose will lead them to another card and so on.
4 Each card is read out and the options which it presents are discussed. If done in groups, a great deal of discussion can result as trainees work their way to an end situation.

### VARIATIONS

a Trainees rewrite cards, options, solutions and exits to make existing mazes more relevant or satisfying to them.
b They set new topics for mazes, write new entry situations or write whole mazes for themselves, for other trainees and for you.
c People can write mazes for themselves about past decisions that went wrong. They can write in for themselves choices that were *not* available to them in the past. Working through these new options can be quite healing in its effect.

### RATIONALE/COMMENT

Mazes are a good way of structuring discussions so that trainees are guided to discuss issues or choices chosen by the maze writer. The information is provided. The task is to rally relevant thoughts, exercise judgement and negotiate with others. Mazes also face trainees, in a harmless way, with the effects of their own choices.

ENTRY TO THE MAZE

You're a busy teacher in a Swiss school. You've been teaching for fifteen years and you don't feel as if you've changed much in the last ten. You're tired and rather bored with your job. Your choices are:
a) Leave the teaching profession (see Card 1).
b) Take an RSA (DOTE) course (see Card 2).
c) Go on as you are (see Card 3).

---

**1**

Who's going to employ a tired, middle-aged ex-teacher? Unless you've got a private income, I suggest you think again!

EXIT OR RETURN

---

**5**

So, you're a quitter are you? Well, then, you're back at the entry to the maze except that now you feel as if you've failed at something too. Wouldn't you like to think again?

EXIT OR RETURN

---

**2**

You start on the RSA (DOTE) course, but what with the travelling, the Thursday nights and the homework, you find it's really much more work than you'd imagined. Your choices are:
a) Talk to the tutors (see Card 4).
b) Drop out (see Card 5).
c) Sigh and keep going (see Card 6).

---

**6**

You keep going but after a while you have the feeling that everybody else is doing better than you. Your choices are:
a) Keep quiet about it (see Card 7).
b) Tell the tutors (see Card 8).
c) Talk to the other students about it (see Card 9).

---

**3**

Well, you'll just get more and more bored, frustrated with your classes and boring to those around you. Do you really want to age that fast?

EXIT OR RETURN

---

**7**

You suffer in silence but things don't get any better. You're driven mad with jealousy and despair. What are you going to do?

RETURN?

---

**4**

The tutors are sympathetic and try not to overload you, but basically they just tell you to keep going.

GO BACK TO CARD 2

---

**8**

The tutors are very encouraging and keep telling you that you're doing all right, but you don't really believe them. You still feel bad.

RETURN?

---

Fig. 7 Example maze for in-service trainees

---

**9**

You're amazed to find that a lot of the other trainees feel exactly the same way as you. You talk about it, feel reassured, and decide to do more groupwork.

MOVE TO CARD 10

---

**10**

You keep going on the course and try to keep up. You meet a lot of new ideas. Your choices are:

a) Try all the ideas out on your students exactly as they were taught to you on the course (see Card 11).

b) Tell your colleagues at work about the ideas at every opportunity you get (see Card 12).

c) Not try anything new (see Card 13).

d) Take the ideas you like, adapt them to fit your situation, try them out and adapt them again if necessary (see Card 14).

---

**11**

A lot of the ideas don't seem to work as well in your classes as they did on the course. You've forgotten quite why you're doing them and your class is stunned anyway by the sudden bombardment of strange ideas. Confusion. Lack of confidence.

DEAD END

---

**12**

Your colleagues at work become bored with and defensive at your enthusiastic ramblings about 'DOTE – this' and 'RSA – that'. You find yourself increasingly isolated in the staffroom and amongst your colleagues. The head of department becomes wary of you.

DEAD END

---

**13**

Well, you've stayed at the entry to the maze really, haven't you? Plus . . . it's doubtful if you'll get through the exam!

DEAD END

---

**14**

You gain confidence gradually as you adopt and adapt more and more ideas. Your class gains confidence as they find they can communicate more and more successfully in English. Things are looking up.

MOVE TO CARD 15

---

**15**

Your techniques improve. Your language improves. Your classes improve. But then the RSA exam looms up before you! Your feelings are:

a) 'I hope I pass' (see Card 16).

b) 'I'm sure I'll fail' (see Card 17).

c) 'Well . . . whether I pass or fail I'll have learned something anyway' (see Card 18).

---

**16**

Then you'll have another piece of paper in your pocket, which is good. Perhaps more important is what you feel you have personally gained as a result of the course.

EXIT

---

**17**

Then you won't have that piece of paper in your pocket. But perhaps you'll feel that you've learnt a lot for yourself that will help your work as a teacher.

EXIT

---

**Fig. 7** Continued

```
                      18
        You finish the course. Your career has
        been refreshed. You think you might be
        able to make it through the next few
        years with increased interest.
                                      EXIT
```

**Fig. 7** Continued

ACKNOWLEDGEMENT/READING

The above maze is taken from *Models and Metaphors in Language Teacher Training* Woodward (CUP, 1991). I first learnt about reading mazes from Mario Rinvolucri. See Berer and Rinvolucri (1981), Farthing (1981) and Woodward (1988a and 1991).

# CORRECTING MISTAKES IN INFORMATION

## Preparation

Find or produce an information source that has a lot of mistakes in it. For example:

- texts where stages, phases, methods, techniques and so forth are wrongly named or defined,
- handouts that don't agree with the lecture they accompany,
- lists of exponents that don't fit the named functions,
- awful teaching demonstrations,
- transcriptions of lessons full of meaningless language,
- visual aids that are bad for their stated purpose,
- activities that do not practise what they set out to practise,
- simplistic or misleading grammar explanations,
- written work or a tape of students or trainees which is flawed or debatable in some way.

## Procedure

Ask the trainees to correct the information orally, mentally or in writing. The trainees can do the work in class, with others, or as a self-access activity.

### RATIONALE/COMMENT

**a** Reshaping and amending work which is already done can sometimes be easier than starting from scratch. It certainly appeals to those with critical natures.

**b** If *you* made the mistakes, being corrected by trainees can be a good role change.

**c** Trainees prove to themselves that they do know what is correct.

**3.8**

**MATERIALS**
See Preparation

**TRAINEES**
Any

# Section 3: Mostly after

3.9

**MATERIALS**
Sets of matching
information (see
below)

**TRAINEES**
Any

# MATCHING

## Preparation

Take sources of information that can be split into halves that match in some way. If used for self-access, all the material needs to be jumbled and made available to each trainee. If trainees work in pairs, then one partner has one half of the information and the other has the other half.

Below is an example. The left-hand column in the example lists some listening micro-skills that could be very useful to language students. The right-hand column lists types of listening material and tasks that could be used in class to practise different micro-skills. Each item in the left-hand column can be matched up with an item in the right-hand column. For example, item 3 mentions material and a task that could be used to practise micro-skill A. Thus, the left- and right-hand columns complement each other but are out of sequence with respect to each other.

### Example matching sheet

List of micro-skills in listening

Type of material and task

A Picking out discourse signals such as 'First . . . ' and 'To move on a bit . . . '

1 A tape of a three-minute conversation. The task is to state how many people were talking and what about.

B Understanding the gist of an extended conversation.

2 A taped dialogue. The teacher stops the tape often and asks students what word comes next.

C Summarising mentally so that recall and comparison are effective in listening to long stretches of speech.

3 A tape of a lecture. The accompanying sheet contains a large number of signpost words. The task is to tick the ones heard in the lecture.

D Predicting what might come up next in terms of content.

4 The first half of a conversation. Students listen and then discuss what points might come up in the second half.

E Knowing what class of word should follow at any point and in what form.

5 Short stretches of talk. After each stretch, a student has to recap briefly in their own words.

© Longman Group UK Ltd 1992

Matching sheets like the one above can be given out on one sheet of paper for individuals to consider or for pairs to work on together. Alternatively, each item labelled with a letter and each item labelled with a number could be cut up separately and handed out at random to the class.

## Procedure

1 Trainees read the sets of material and try to match them up. If the trainees have all the data on one sheet, they do this individually at home or in class. Alternatively, if the items on the sheet have been cut up, trainees have different pieces of information and work together at matching the items up.
2 There is a final check. This can be done by handing out 'key' sheets or by asking trainees to report what they've matched up and why.

### VARIATIONS

a Very different subjects can be matched. For example:
  ● professional terminology can be matched to stress bubbles, e.g:

  ● steps in a lesson plan can be matched to extracts from lesson transcripts,
  ● sample language exercises from coursebooks can be matched to theoretical approaches,
  ● a series of classroom seating diagrams can be matched to steps in a lesson.

### RATIONALE/COMMENT

Apart from the preparation time, the activity moves swiftly, since it tests trainees' understanding rather than asks them to produce anything new.

## SEQUENCING

### Preparation

1 Take any information source that has a proper sequence that the trainees are likely to know because it has been taught on the course. For example, the stages of a lesson of a particular type (see example below), the headings of a lesson plan of a certain kind, the parts of a particular substitution table, the steps of a certain activity, or the words or phrases in a sentence they are familiar with.
2 Write the steps out in the usual order.
3 Make the same number of copies as you have trainees. Then make an extra copy.
4 Keep the extra copy as a master.
5 Cut each of the other copies into strips. Jumble them, then keep them together in an envelope or with a paper clip so you don't lose any! The list overleaf is of the steps of an oral inductive presentation.

**3.10**

**MATERIALS**
Copies of an information source which can be reordered once jumbled up

**TRAINEES**
Any

**CONTENT**
Any which includes sequences of some kind

### Example list for sequencing

- Find out what your students need to learn.
- Do research into the target item.
- Think of a suitable situation for the language.
- Choose presentation aids (pictures, tape, etc.).
- Build up the situation with the students.
- Check the situation is understood.
- Ask some concept questions to guide students towards the meaning of the target item.
- Elicit or give an example of the target item.
- Give a clear oral model.
- Highlight the spoken form of the target item.
- Say the model sentence again naturally.
- Ask concept questions to check understanding.

© Longman Group UK Ltd 1992

## Procedure

**1** Trainees attempt to put the steps into a sensible sequence. They can do this individually or in pairs; at home or in class; while watching a lesson or listening to a tape of one; or from memory.

**2** Trainees check the order by calling out their version or by checking against a list on an OHP or board.

**3** Differences of opinion are discussed.

### RATIONALE/COMMENT

By receiving data in the wrong order and being asked to put it into a better order, trainees are more likely to think out the rationale behind certain sequences rather than to learn the steps off by heart.

## 3.11

**MATERIAL**
None

**TRAINEES**
Any

# SUMMARISING

## Procedure

**1** After working with some information, trainees summarise its content. They can do this by, for example:

   **a** making a title or writing sub- or side headings (if the information source is a text),

   **b** teaching the contents to someone else,

   **c** drawing a mind map or branching diagram of the key points,

   **d** deciding on, say, ten key words that sum up the spirit of the piece,

   **e** writing an aim for a lesson plan without an aim written on it,

   **f** producing a graph, diagram or series of pictures.

**VARIATION**

Summaries can work the other way round, for example, trainees can start from summaries, research them, and then expand them.

**RATIONALE/COMMENT**

In order to make a good summary, trainees have to understand the gist of the information, pick out the main points, and leave behind the redundant or less important points. This involves thorough interaction with the information.

# CATEGORISING

## Procedure

**3.12**

**MATERIALS**
A large pool of items of some sort (examples below).

**TRAINEES**
Any

1 Ask trainees to create or read or look through a pool of items, for example:
   - a list of visual aids,
   - a list of advantages and disadvantages of deductive presentations,
   - examples of different classroom activities,
   - examples of different kinds of drills,
   - examples of different kinds of listening material, etc.

   (There is a full example list below.)

2 Ask trainees to classify or categorise the items in the pool according to any criteria they like as long as they can explain their criteria later. This can be done at home or in class with others.

3 Ask trainees to give their categories names.

4 The trainees record their results in notebooks, on OHP transparencies or on posters so that everyone can see the different ways people have named and categorised the pool of items.

**VARIATION**

If working with lists, transfer the items in the list onto separate pieces of card so that they can be moved around, ordered and reordered as trainees investigate new ways of categorising the information. Alternatively, if you have asked *trainees* to create the pool of items, they can themselves write each one on a separate slip of paper.

**RATIONALE/COMMENT**

a Categorising information and naming the categories helps trainees impose their own view on the information.

b Seeing other people's ways of breaking down and organising data is a good reminder of how different people are.

Example worksheet with a list of items for categorising by trainees

Here are some methods/approaches in language teaching/learning that we have read about and discussed on the course. Read through them and then group them into two to four categories according to any criteria you like. Name each category and be prepared to give others an account of your reasoning for the categories *and* their names.

| | |
|---|---|
| Situational Teaching | The Silent Way |
| Total Physical Response | The Direct Method |
| Behaviourism | Eclecticism |
| Counselling Learning | Suggestopaedia |
| Notional-functionalism | Activity-based Teaching |
| The Natural Approach | The Task-based Approach |
| The Audio-lingual Method | All's Well |
| Free Conversation | Immersion Learning |
| Grammar Translation | Subject-based Teaching |

© Longman Group UK Ltd 1992

## 3.13

**MATERIALS**
Two separate resources or sets of information

**TRAINEES**
Any

## SAME OR DIFFERENT?

## Procedure

Ask trainees to compare two resources or sets of information and say whether and in what ways they feel the two sets are the same or different. Here are some examples of things that can be compared:

- assignments on the same topic done by different trainees,
- a lesson plan and a lesson,
- a trainee's ideas for teaching a page of a textbook compared to the ideas in the teacher's book,
- two pieces of student written work marked by different people,
- tapes of the same conversation featuring students with different mother tongues,
- the language that has been presented early in a lesson and the language actually used by the students in the practice activities,
- the ways two particular students participate in class, or the ways they like to learn.

**RATIONALE/COMMENT**

**a** Trainees get to know both things better by discussing and comparing them.

**b** Similarities or differences may be unexpected (e.g. one coursebook gives a range of fourteen different phrases for expressing disagreement with an opinion while native speakers on a particular radio programme only used one, 'Yeah, but . . . ').

# STRUCTURING DISCUSSIONS

## Procedure

After receiving some information, trainees discuss it. This can happen one-to-one with the trainer, or with a peer, or in small groups. You can structure discussion by asking participants to:

- recap the basics of the content,
- recap the basics of the process whereby the content is conveyed,
- debate the pros and cons of the content in more or less formal ways,
- discuss what changes would have to be made before the content could be applied to trainees' own circumstances,
- discuss personal opinions of the information,
- prepare questions for each other or for you,
- memorise the main points by walking around, rehearsing them out loud, and testing each other in a mingling promenade,
- discussing the rules, principles or implications suggested by the information,
- discussing a topic and planning an essay based on the information,
- using the information to solve a problem,
- analysing and evaluating the information,
- thinking up the opposite of all the arguments and ideas given in the material.

### VARIATIONS

**a** All groups can have the same task or different groups can have different tasks according to interest, need, experience and so on.

**b** Discussion can occur immediately (which favours the fast reactors) or after a delay (to encourage more considered discussion).

### RATIONALE/COMMENT

Talking about something after you have experienced it is extremely natural, and choosing from a large repertoire of discussion structures can enable you and the group to sustain or raise interest levels.

READING
UTMU (1976 pp. 40–61).

**3.14**

**MATERIALS**
Something fairly interesting, dense or provocative to discuss

**TRAINEES**
Any

# UNPLANNED SPACE

## Procedure

1 When you plan for trainees to do some kind of work on an information source, follow it in the timetable with an unplanned slot of at least an hour long. Do not prepare *anything* at all in the way of input for that session.

2 Give them plenty of advanced notice that there will be a 'question corner' or 'unplanned space' session. Ask them to bring questions on anything that has happened so far in the training course.

**3.15**

**MATERIALS**
None

**TRAINEES**
Any

3 Run the session in an informal, relaxed way. Trainees can ask questions of each other and/or you. Allow plenty of silence and time for people to think.

4 When it seems that no more questions are coming from the trainees, ask them questions. The spirit of these questions needs to be gentle. This can be your way of checking that trainees really have understood different parts of the course.

### RATIONALE/COMMENT

a If trainees are continually fed new material without a break, they can begin to feel rather pressurised. If they know there is a definite space specially for questions and comments, they may feel less panicked when meeting new material afterwards on the course.

b *Totally* unplanned space will allow people time to leave, go shopping, sleep, walk, have a bath . . . The work they have done will settle and brew in its own way inside each participant.

## 3.16

**MATERIALS**
None

**TRAINEES**
Any

# SILENT REFLECTION TIME

## Procedure

1 In an input session, once trainees have had some information and have had time to ask questions and comment, give them a few minutes of silent reflection time.

2 Suggest that they think (not look!) through the material they have met so far and see if they can (a) remember it and (b) make sense of it. Again, ask them *not* to look through their notes during this time.

3 Sit and do the same thing yourself. This should help you to allow a realistic length of time for the task and not jump in too soon with a new activity.

4 It is important that you do not stop the silent reflection time in a loud or abrupt way. Perhaps give gentle warning messages like, 'Just a few minutes more . . . ' and finally, 'When you're ready, have a look at your notes' or 'When you feel ready, team up with someone else who is ready and check with each other and your notes to see what you left out of your mental recall.'

### VARIATION

Some people find it difficult to think when in a circle or line of other people in a classroom, so trainees can therefore do their reflecting while standing, walking, staring out of a window, doodling, sitting in the corridor or mumbling to themselves.

### RATIONALE/COMMENT

a People need time to store, recall, make sense of newly encountered material and to integrate it with what they already know. Some people also need a rest from constant listening and talking in order to be with themselves.

**b** People work in different ways and at different speeds. This process allows people time to catch up and do some thinking on their own.

**c** You get a chance to ponder the work so far and to make choices as to the next move.

## TRUE/FALSE STATEMENTS

### Preparation

Choose an information source. Make True/False statements about it.

### Procedure

1 After the trainees have met a body of information, ask them to read and consider a list of True/False statements. They work individually. Here are some True/False statements that could be used after reading Chapter 1, Section 1 of this book:

- There are exactly nine areas to consider when analysing an activity.    T/F
- Brainstorms are the only activities that can be analysed.    T/F
- By altering small details of an activity you can radically affect it.    T/F
- 'Splitting the atom' makes lots of new activities out of one activity.    T/F

2 The trainees then check with each other to see if they have come to the same conclusions.

#### RATIONALE/COMMENT

True/False statements can cut through long passages of complex instructions to consolidate basic facts. They also force trainees to commit themselves to a point of view and see how much they have understood.

**3.17**

**MATERIALS**
True/False statements and an information source

**TRAINEES**
Any

## JIGSAW RESOURCES

### Procedure

1 Divide the resource up into two or more different pieces.
2 Divide the trainees up into the same number of groups.
3 Give piece A of the resource to the people in group A and piece B to the people in group B, and so on.
4 See that each group has come to terms with its piece of the information source.
5 Next, pair one person from group A with one from group B and so on for all the participants. Give the pairs a task or some questions that can only be completed if partners pool what they know.
6 Check that the task has been completed well.

**3.18**

**MATERIALS**
A text, tape, video or other resource divided up into two or more different parts; copies of a task sheet

**TRAINEES**
Any

## VARIATIONS

**a** Jigsaws can involve two, three, four, five, or more groups and pieces.

**b** The resource can, in fact, be kept intact or whole and trainees concentrate on different aspects of it. Thus, different trainees read, listen or look for different things in the same text, tape or lesson.

**c** A jigsaw activity can consist of two trainees watching the same technique used in two different classes by two different teachers.

## RATIONALE/COMMENT

**a** You, the trainer, are encouraged to chop up material into assimilable chunks.

**b** Trainees have a chance to check their understanding of a chunk of text (or of reality or experience) with others.

**c** Everyone has something to say and there is a need to speak in order to complete a task.

**d** Jigsaws use a variety of different channels, e.g. visual (reading) and auditory (talking and listening), and thus can appeal to trainees with different dominant sensory modes.

READING
Hess (1991 pp. 104–115) offers additional extensions to the basic jigsaw idea.

## 3.19

**MATERIALS**
Little file cards and a small cardboard box for each trainee

**TRAINEES**
Any

# WHAT *EXACTLY* ARE YOU READING?

## Procedure

1 Set trainees the following task for whenever they read an article or part of a book, and *before* they give the book back:
'Write on a card the following information: author's surname, author's intials, date of publication, title of text, name of publisher, place of publication, volume, issue and page numbers of the part you read.'

2 Encourage each participant to keep all her cards together, in alphabetical order, in a little box.

## EXTENSION

3 Trainees write quotes, comments or mini-reviews on the backs of the cards.

## RATIONALE/COMMENT

**a** The trainee will be able to find the details of the books and articles again if necessary.

**b** Source references in the trainees' written work are more likely to be given correctly. This means that original authors get credit and interested readers can find these sources more easily.

**c** The trainees learn a method of working that may be useful later, for example, when studying for a (higher) degree. Not keeping good records can involve people wasting hours in the library trying to refind things they read months before.

**d** If trainees do the extension, they summarise and evaluate what they have learned from reading. This may help understanding and recall and can be useful to others who borrow the cards and who have had no time to do the full reading.

# TEACHER RESPONSES TO DIFFICULT SITUATIONS

## Procedure

**1** Give everyone a sheet of paper with a description of a problematic teaching situation on it. Each person has a *different* situation. For example, one trainee might have 'My students get bored during oral drills', another might have 'I have to set lots of written work in my school but I don't have time to correct it.'

**2** Ask trainees to mingle, and to interview each other as to a possible strategy for use in the situation.

**3** Each person notes down the strategies they are offered by the others. They also make a note of who offered each strategy, thus: 'Jane – Try to ad lib more', 'Sarah – Pay more attention to visualisation; remember what we learned about Stevick's ideas in *Images and Options*.' (Note: each trainee does this about a different situation.)

**4** Each person sits down and reads through the strategies they are offered. They then write down the advantages and disadvantages for each one.

**5** Everyone reports back to the whole group on their situation, strategies, and advantages and disadvantages. There is general discussion throughout this stage.

### VARIATIONS

**a** Starter situations can be thought up by the trainees.

**b** Trainees work on situations initially as homework or as a self-access task before soliciting other people's comments and suggestions.
Finally, they each write a report on their situation, again as homework or self-access, adding in the comment and solutions they have thought up and received.

### RATIONALE/COMMENT

In any teaching situation there are many possible actions, reactions and strategies to choose from. This training process reinforces an awareness of this plethora of options.

### ACKNOWLEDGEMENT/READING

I got the basic idea from Gerry Kenny and Bonnie Tsai. See their regular column 'Teachers Speak Out' in *PET Magazine* for examples of particular teacher problems and advice.

**3.20**

**MATERIALS**
A sheet of paper for each trainee; each sheet bears a description of a different problematic teaching situation

**TRAINEES**
Any

## CHAPTER 4

# *Moving on from input*

This chapter presents training processes which are designed to encourage trainer and trainees to internalise newly met information by memorising, physically storing, visualising and (re)organising it. Other choices of training process here encourage transformation of the information by using it in new situations and adapting it for the learners' own purposes.

## 4.1

**MATERIALS**
None

**TRAINEES**
Any

## TIME TO MEMORISE

### Procedure

1 Allow time within a training session for people to work on memorising material. Some people will want to do this by writing out the material again by hand using coloured pens and highlighters. Some will want to do this by rote, applying such learning techniques as muttering, chanting or walking about and talking to themselves. Some will want to read the material quietly and then get into pairs to test each other by asking questions. Others will want to go through the material mentally, that is, mentally saying it and acting it out, seeing it in their mind's eye or hearing it again and again, and periodically checking against the material to see what they remembered and what

they forgot. Others will want to make up mnemonics in the form of acronyms, little stories, pictures and mental visualisation. Some may want to make wall posters that they can glance at later from time to time, for long-term peripheral learning.

2 Ask people to describe to each other their particular methods of 'stamping' material in and give them time in each session to memorise things.

### RATIONALE/COMMENT

This process gives people time, public space and new ideas for memorising material instead of considering memorising as old-fashioned or as somehow taking care of itself.

# MAPPING THE WORK DONE

## Procedure

1 After an input session, workshop or self-access session is over, trainees gather, after a break, on a volunteer basis in an informal setting, with the trainer present.

2 The group uses a number of techniques to recap what has happened in the session (see ideas below).

3 Some trainees will not want to come to the recapping meetings; in fact, some may find these sessions annoying. But other trainees, who perhaps have a fear of forgetting or who enjoy thinking back and reorganising data, will turn up regularly to these 'mapping' sessions.

4 Use a different idea each time, for a maximum of twenty minutes each session.

5 Once trainees have got the idea, ask them for their own ideas on remembering, reordering, reframing and relearning the work and try those out too.

6 It's important not to go on for too long and not to hurry.

7 Don't take in written work or correct anything. Let people (including yourself!) do the work in their own way.

8 If, on some days, people don't feel like mapping, don't force it.

### SOME DIFFERENT WAYS OF MAPPING

a Individuals list and note down in chronological order the main events/activities of the day by remembering out loud as a group. 'Didn't that come before the listening activity?' 'Oh, I thought that was later.'

b Again using the group memory, individuals list the events of the day backwards, that is, from the most recent to the first.

c Each trainee writes down the key words and phrases (maximum ten) which sum up the main points or feelings of the day. They then share these by telling the whole group (if it's a small one) or by talking in pairs.

**4.2**

**MATERIALS**
None

**TRAINEES**
Any who need space and time to get their thoughts organised before they feel like dealing with any more new material

d Everyone remembers one thing from the day and shares this with the others. This thing can be the one that is most (or least) interesting/ memorable/likeable/strange for them.

e Each participant draws a mind map of the day (or session etc.) using the same central seed word but with any organisation of branches they wish (see 2.13 *The mind-map lecture*). People then look at each others' mind maps and add anything they wish to their own.

f The group recalls the content of the day and then tries to recall the processes involved, that is, *how* the ideas, opinions or pieces of information were transmitted.

g You talk with the group about your decisions, choices, problems and pleasures from the day's work.

h The group, after remembering the main content blocks and processes of the day, compiles a list of the *implications* of what they have learned for their own teaching situation.

### RATIONALE/COMMENT

a Some trainees, especially on intensive courses, feel their heads are swimming with ideas. Mapping sessions help those who need to ponder and organise what has gone on.

b Using a variety of strategies for recapping and consolidating gives everyone new strategies to try out later when the group no longer exists.

READING
Woodward 1989d.

## 4.3

**MATERIALS**
Poster-making materials

**TRAINEES**
Any

## POSTER SUMMARIES

### Procedure

1 After a group discussion, lecture or review session, homework, reading or other work, give out poster-making materials (e.g. cheap brown paper or the back of wallpaper; coloured marker pens, crayons and paintbrushes; Blu-tack or pins; scissors; glue) and ask trainees to produce (individually, in pairs or in groups) a poster summarising their findings. The posters will all be different. They can include cut out pictures, captions, headlines, speech bubbles or anything else.

2 Trainees put the posters up for everyone to see. People walk round and look at them. This phase can have many different variations, for example:

a A member or members of each group can stand by their poster and answer questions or elaborate on it.

b Everybody promenades at once and then there is an open question time when questions are taken on one poster at a time.

c Groups nominate a 'runner' who goes to the posters, reads them and carries information back to the group.

**d** Each poster has a message board near it for people's comments and questions about the poster.

**EXTENSION**

**3** The posters can be used as prompts for oral presentations.

**RATIONALE/COMMENT**

**a** Making a poster helps people to clarify and summarise ideas.

**b** A poster is a durable reminder of a day's or session's work.

**c** Posters are eye-catching and fun to make.

**d** Making a poster doesn't demand as much confidence as doing an oral presentation.

**e** People can walk away from a poster if it bores them.

ACKNOWLEDGEMENT/READING

Thanks to the English Teachers Association of Switzerland who suggested I make a poster for their first national conference. I did and I liked doing it! See Sturtridge (1987), Allwright (1984) and Marks (1989).

# TEACHER HOMEWORK IDEAS

## Procedure

**4.4**

**MATERIALS**
None

**TRAINEES**
Any, although some ideas (e.g. b and c) are only useful for in-service trainees

The basic idea here is for trainees to undertake some private research in their own time, using easily available resources in an open-ended way. Here are some examples:

**a** After a seminar on listening comprehension, give trainees the following homework:

'Between now and our next meeting, keep your ears open for a conversation in which you are not involved and on which you can safely eavesdrop. Tune into what is being said, listening for content. This may not be easy, but be patient. As you get used to the speakers' voices, pay attention to their intonation, their manner and the way they express themselves.'

At the start of the next meeting, trainees form small groups and discuss what the exercise brought to their attention.

**b** After a seminar on adapting textbooks, try the next homework:

'You are fed up with your current coursebook, but the fact is that you are required to cover its contents for examination purposes. Look at the next unit in the coursebook and make a list of the structures, vocabulary, etc. which are presented. Take a newspaper in the target language and seek examples of this structure or vocabulary. Teach the next unit using examples from the newspaper rather than from the textbook. Tell the group how it went.'

**c** Or:

'Next time your students are busily working without you, look at them and imagine that they are your teachers. How would they teach you? How would you feel being taught by them?'

**OTHER VARIATIONS**

Teacher homework can involve experimenting with eye contact, guessing how long periods of time have been, remembering past teachers, writing definitions of the words *teacher* and *student*, finding out what encourages a friend most in conversation.

**RATIONALE/COMMENT**

a These sorts of exercises can be used as lead-ins or follow-ups to course input or as personal homework for a teacher not on a course.

b The activities get trainees thinking independently about important issues outside course time.

c Teacher homework does not involve you in lots of marking or the trainees in tedious and time-consuming copying up of notes into essay form.

ACKNOWLEDGEMENTS/READING

This work comes from Bonnie Tsai and Gerry Kenny. See Kenny (1986a and b).

## 4.5

**MATERIALS**
None

**TRAINEES**
Any

# REVIEW CIRCLES

## Procedure

1 Ask trainees to stand and form two concentric circles. There should be an equal number of people in both. The inside people should face out and the outside people should face in, so that everyone has a partner in the other circle.

2 Agree on a signal such as the lights being switched on and off or a bell sounding. Ask people to stop talking when you use this signal.

3 Next, ask trainees to talk to their partner in the other circle to make sure that they can remember, for example, what 'gist' listening is.

4 Once you think people have had time to do this, use the pre-arranged signal.

5 Once people have stopped talking, ask the outside circle people to move round one place to the left. The inner circle people stay where they are.

6 Now, set a new task, for example, ask people to check with their new partner the meaning of the word *collocation*.

7 Use the signal and ask the outside people to move round again one place to the left. The activity goes on in this way for as long as people like. I find five or six changes about right.

8 People go back to their seats and, referring to their course notes, check anything they found difficult to recall.

**VARIATIONS**

a Either the inner or outer circle people can move and either to the left or to the right . . . but be consistent!

**b** The tasks can begin: 'Explain the meaning of . . .', 'Explain the difference between . . .', 'Remember all you can about . . .', 'List the ten . . .', 'Explain why you would . . .', etc.

**c** In large groups or in difficult spaces, use more than one set of concentric circles.

### RATIONALE/COMMENT

**a** More may be remembered if material is reviewed with a partner.

**b** This· is a review rather than a test. The atmosphere is of relaxed remembering rather than stressful examination.

**c** Trainees are, initially, well away from their notebooks and so they have to rely on memory. Going back to their notebooks afterwards to check up on forgotten items means more targeted and motivated reading of their notes.

# VISUALISING PHYSICAL ROUTINES

## 4.6

**MATERIALS**
None

**TRAINEES**
Those unfamiliar with a particular teaching or classroom management routine

**CONTENT**
Routines with an element of physical movement

Sometimes trainees will be introduced to a classroom routine which involves the teacher in moving, gesturing, making eye contact and handling teaching aids. For example:
- starting a choral drill and moving to individual drills,
- building a dialogue using pictures and elicitation from students,
- question and answer work in the sequence: (1) teacher to individual student, (2) student to teacher, (3) student to student directed, (4) student to student in open pairs, one pair at a time, across the class and then (5) student to student in closed pairs.

Once you feel the trainees have understood the reasons for the routine and its steps, ask them to practise it by doing a dry run before they try it out with a real class.

## Procedure

1 Remind trainees or elicit from them the steps of the routine you want to review with them. As they call out the steps, mime them or use appropriate gestures. So, if working on choral drilling, you might ask, 'What comes first?' Trainees might call out, 'Attract the students' attention.' You show them how you would do that by, for example, glancing around the room to make eye contact, motioning to people with 'sh' and listening (hand behind your ear) or whatever you would normally do. Ask, 'What comes next?' Trainees might say, 'Say the model sentence.' You mime doing that. And so on.

2 Once you have reviewed the whole routine, ask trainees to find a space for themselves, turn away from the other trainees and face the wall, door or a window. This way they will have some private space and will not see each other's actions.

3 Next, ask trainees to go through the routine at their own speed, without talking but *acting it out* by using natural gesture, eye contact and so on to an imaginary class in front of them.

N.B. Find something to occupy yourself – do anything except sit and stare at trainees.

4 Allow plenty of time for people to forget, remember, rerun and slowly work their way, physically, through the routine.

5 When most people seem to have finished, ask them to sit down and check against their notes to see if they remembered everything. Keep your eye contact away from the group.

6 When everyone has had a chance to finish and check against their notes, ask different individuals if there are any stages they tended to leave out. Suggest they do some more acting in a quiet place away from people, perhaps at home. Tell people that top skiers use acting out with visualisation to perfect complex movements down a run, and that it is a standard form of athletics practice nowadays.

### VARIATIONS

a Trainees sit, close their eyes and go through the routine mentally without much physical movement.

b Trainees sitting, with their eyes closed, imagine themselves going through a routine such as one of the ones mentioned above and, finally, imagine having completed it *successfully*.

c You can talk the trainees through the routine while they are imagining.

d To raise confidence before a real class, trainees can visualise a scene where they successfully taught something to somebody.

### RATIONALE/COMMENT

a Trainees are given time to mentally and physically work through a routine unobserved, thus gaining practice in an unstressful environment.

b This training process makes use of body memory and thus opens the way to synthesis of mental and physical recollection.

ACKNOWLEDGEMENT
I learnt all the variations from Herbert Puchta.

## 4.7

MATERIALS
Different for
different
assignments

TRAINEES
Any

# ASSIGNMENTS OPTIONS

## Procedure

Ask trainees to produce an essay, a taped talk, a checklist, answers to questions or to complete a cloze text, gather data, or do any other type of assignment based on course input and experience.

### VARIATIONS

a Negotiate the assignment types and titles with trainees.

**b** Give the assignments out all at once at the start of a course or one by one. Set a different deadline for each assignment or just one final hand-in date for the lot.

**c** In your instructions include: reading references, a couple of sentences written down as a guide to the style to be followed, a word count, approximate period of suggested study time, checklists of important points to cover, and guidelines on how to structure the work.

**d** Give trainees an explanation of how assignments are to be marked, corrected, graded or commented on and by what criteria they will be judged.

**e** Ask the trainees to include lies in their work. This keeps the readers more awake and can be great fun.

**f** Link input very clearly to assignments (e.g. 'Listen carefully now because the next part will be useful for your second assignment'). You can link assignments to teaching practice too.

**g** Allow time during the course for study, for group note-taking and discussion of assignments.

**h** All trainees do the same assignments or different (groups of) trainees do different assignments or different aspects of the same assignment.

**i** Trainees can do assignments at different times from each other.

**j** Try assigning a role play essay, for example:
'You are a traditional student who likes overt grammar work in class, lots of homework and clear grades. Write a letter to your language school explaining your reasons for being dissatisfied with your teacher who . . .'

**k** Similarly structured work can be gained by giving trainees instructions such as:
    'In your answer you should (i) define x, y and z, (ii) give the source, and explain the reasoning behind the quotation ". . .", (iii) select some (e.g.) listening activities and explain the reasons for your selection, and (iv) comment on. . .'
    Other key verbs in your instructions could be *relate, compare, contrast, design,* and *produce.*

**RATIONALE/COMMENT**

Assignments give trainees a chance for sustained recap, research and production of information new to them. Trainees can achieve a more concentrated overview of recent work, and this may lead them to develop new links or insights. Assignments give trainees something to work towards and something to keep afterwards.

READING
Gibbs et al (1984).

## 4.8

**MATERIALS**
Different for the
different ideas

**TRAINEES**
Any

# ASSIGNMENT MARKING OPTIONS
## Procedure

Perhaps the most normal way of marking assignments is: (1) the trainer takes in all the assignments; (2) the trainer ploughs through the lot, adding comments and grades; (3) the assignments are handed back to individual trainees who may or may not wish to disclose their comments/grades to others.

Once an assignment has been drafted or completed the following ideas can be used to improve it or check it.

**a** Trainees compare their assignments with a list (provided by you) of points that need to come up under the question. You can write up the list before, during or after reading all the assignments.

**b** Before you or the trainees read and comment on the assignments, they can brainstorm and then prioritise the sort of criticism, marking or comments they would like on their work.

**c** Trainees compare their assignments with those commented on in an examiner's report from the previous year.

**d** A panel, consisting of a group of trainees on the same course, reads and discusses completed assignments and negotiates marks for each.

**e** Assignments can have corrections and comments written straight onto the body of the text or on a separate sheet. Or you can ask trainees to leave a space at the bottom or side margin(s) on each page for comments. Alternatively, ask them to use triple-space typing or double-space handwriting.

**f** Comments on assignments need not be in red, they can be in different colours or in pencil. The use of different colours is especially helpful if more than one person (e.g. a tutor and another trainee) is commenting.

**g** Comments can be in the form of questions to which the trainee has to reply.

**h** Photocopy the best bits of different assignments to make a collage for display.

**i** Once you have marked and handed back the assignments, give trainees the chance to sit and read through your comments. Then pair the trainees off so that strengths and weaknesses are complemented as far as possible. The pairs then go for a walk *without* the assignments. Their task is to discuss where they think they went right and wrong in their assignments.

**RATIONALE/COMMENT**

Creative, positive marking of assignments can change an assignment experience from one of dread, stress and lonely failure to one of interest, learning and peer support.

ACKNOWLEDGEMENT/READING
Variation (b) I read in Gibbs *et al* (1984). Variation (f) I learnt from Marion Williams.

# METHODOLOGY NOTEBOOKS
## Procedure

**4.9**

**MATERIALS**
One envelope
folder, notebook or
other storage
system for each
trainee

**TRAINEES**
Any

At the start of the course, encourage trainees to keep a methodology notebook. You can reinforce this by
- allotting a percentage of the marks in the final assessment to the notebook work,
- making constant reference to the notebooks,
- handing out articles that can be kept in them,
- suggesting ways the notebooks can be kept,
- allowing time for their completion,
- taking them in regularly for perusal and in order to get an idea of what further guidance is necessary.

Things that can go in the notebooks are: notes about materials and exercises used with the trainees on the course, analysis of the processes used by trainers in any language improvement or other sessions, observation sheets filled in by trainees or trainers during or after their own or other people's observed classes.

You can use what you learn from reading the notebooks as the basis for individual tutorials or as starting points for essays, projects, reading assignments, work on particular areas of interest, and class discussions on activities, techniques and materials.

### RATIONALE/COMMENT

Trainees are encouraged to learn from the methodology that is used with them on their training course as well as from course content. This doubles the value of the course as a way of learning about methodology.

READING
Hundleby and Breet (1988).

# TEXTBOOK WRITER'S ROLE PLAY
## Procedure

**4.10**

**MATERIALS**
A different
language
coursebook for
each trainee or
pair of trainees

**TRAINEES**
Any

1 Give (pairs of) trainees a coursebook to teach with or just to look through. Do not let trainees see each other's coursebooks. Make sure that trainees have understood the assumptions about teaching and learning that lie behind the book. Trainees should not tell each other what books they are working on.
2 Ask each trainee to imagine that they are the author of their particular coursebook. They have been invited to a big cocktail party at a book fair. They are to mill around and tell people all about their book without saying its title.
3 Let trainees mingle and talk. They try to guess what particular book or type of book other people are talking about, as well as present their own book in as positive a light as possible.

**4** After about fifteen minutes, ask people who they spoke to, what book they think each person was representing and why they think so.

### VARIATION

Invite other people to the party, such as originators of particular teaching methods (e.g. the Silent Way, Total Physical Response, the Natural Approach, Counselling Learning, the Direct Method, the Grammar/Translation Method and so on). This time conversation is less around the topic of books and more on 'What I like to do in my classes is . . .' and 'My beliefs about learning are . . .'

### RATIONALE/COMMENT

Trainees need to become very familiar with a book or method to be able to activate their learning in this way. Other people asking them questions pushes their learning even further.

ACKNOWLEDGEMENT/READING

Thanks to Denny Packard for telling me about his idea, which is based on Hawley (1974).

## 4.11

**MATERIALS**
Depends on the project

**TRAINEES**
Any

# PROJECTS

## Procedure

**1** Talk with trainees together or individually in order to choose and negotiate an issue or a problem for them to work on.

**2** You and the trainee(s) devise a number of activities such as reading, interviewing, collecting data and materials to help them find a solution to the problem.

**3** Decide on an end product such as a report, a set of lesson plans, a case study, a course design or a dossier of facts and comment. Agree with trainees about who the end product will be presented to (e.g. fellow course participants or you only).

**4** Agree on a time limit longer than one session (anything from one afternoon to three years!).

**5** Agree which stages of the project work you and other trainees will be involved in. The involvement needs to be supportive and advisory rather than directive or competitive.

**6** Trainees can give presentations at several different informal pre-completion meetings so that all trainees can know who is working on what and how things are going, and can offer advice and support.

**7** Trainees present their final product.

### VARIATIONS

**a** Trainees can work on joint projects or ones that are different but related.

**b** Each trainee can present their final product all at once or stage by stage. Projects can be completed orally, via poster or via some other type of presentation or display.

**RATIONALE/COMMENT**

**a** It is important that trainees are very involved in the choice of topic, are supported well throughout, are warned of the self-access nature of the project work and are told how much the project is worth in the overall course assessment.

**b** Trainees are active in this kind of work and responsible for making their own decisions.

**c** You can be in a less authoritarian role and can give advice in a spirit of joint investigation.

**d** Trainees can work at different speeds, in different ways, and in different areas from each other.

READING
UTMU (1976).

# PUBLISHING

This idea really comes from Susan Holden, the editor of *Modern English Teacher*, who has said: 'It's important for teachers who feel they've got something to say to be able to get published. It's quite difficult to get published. I've noticed, certainly with secondary teachers abroad, that they get a terrific amount of confidence from having something they've done in class published in an international magazine. In a sense, it's a form of teacher training.' (Interview with Barry Tomalin, *EFL Gazette*, June 1986).

Since Susan printed the first EFL article I had published, and since this really did make me feel, with great surprise, 'I *can* do it!', I strongly agree with her.

**4.12**

**MATERIALS**
A typewriter or word processor

**TRAINEES**
Any

## Procedure

**1** Encourage trainees who think they might have created a new exercise, technique or something else of potential interest to other language teachers, to write it down clearly as soon as they can in the form of an article.

**2** Encourage them to check some of the main teachers' resource books to make sure their idea isn't already published.

**3** Encourage them to ask some friends and colleagues to read their idea and see if they can understand it. Trainees need to listen carefully to suggestions and incorporate some of them.

**4** Help trainees to do a little research into the number and type of periodicals in the field so that they send the article to one that's appropriate. If they don't, it will be turned down, even if it's brilliant.

**5** The trainee needs to keep a copy of the article and a copy of the letter she writes to the magazine or journal editor, offering to make any changes necessary and asking to receive a copy of any changes the editor makes *before* the idea goes to print.

**6** They send the letter off and wait and see.

### RATIONALE/COMMENT

**a** This encourages trainees to: be aware of what they create in teaching; do research into other people's ideas; communicate their ideas clearly; work with colleagues on ideas.

**b** The idea can be kept wholly private or can be shared with colleagues. If the idea works and if the trainee is successful in getting published, confidence is boosted. If unsuccessful, nothing has really been lost.

## 4.13

**MATERIALS**
Photocopies of any jargon generator

**TRAINEES**
Any

# THE JARGON GENERATOR

## Procedure

1 After trainees have been wading through a lot of reading or input and are starting to complain or make jokes about the amount of terminology they have to learn, show them a jargon generator. There is an example of one (from Woodward 1987a) in Figure 8.

2 Have some fun producing pompous and pretentious sentences with the jargon generator. Suggest that trainees make one of their own too, with terminology from the course.

3 Allow a little time for people to start recalling recent terminology from, for example, error analysis or discourse analysis sessions, and organising it into a similar substitution table. Alternatively, set this as an optional homework and pin up on a noticeboard the one with the most phrases in most columns and which generates the most pretentious sentences.

### RATIONALE/COMMENT

**a** If trainees collect the phrases, play with them and say them out loud, they get better acquainted with them and the terminology may become less threatening.

**b** The activity is iconoclastic and fun.

## 1ST LINE

a range of key

| effective | long-term | inductive | initial | technique-based | bottom-up | teacher-centred |
|---|---|---|---|---|---|---|
| appropriate | short-term | deductive | in-service | text-based | top-down | student-centred |
| optimal | medium-term | evaluative | pre-service | data-based | low-down | learner-centred |
| experiential | | societal | inset | | right-brain | |
| quantitative | | systemic | post-service | | | |
| | | cognitive | | | | |
| | | effective | | | | |
| | | affective | | | | |

## 2ND LINE

self-assessing
awareness-raising
networking

| multiplier effect | high-profile | EFL | course types | within a | given frame |
|---|---|---|---|---|---|
| cascade effect | low-profile | ESL | models | | known frame |
| spillover effect | | TESOL | strategies | | |
| | | ESP | concepts | | |
| | | EAP | modules | | |
| | | NOR | agents | | |
| | | | components | | |
| | | | criteria | | |
| | | | innovations | | |

## 3RD LINE

and in a

| known | teacher-education | context |
|---|---|---|
| related | teacher-development | |
| given | teacher-training | |

Fig. 8 The jargon generator

## 4.14

**MATERIALS**
Poster equipment,
reading list,
dictionaries

**TIME**
Preparation plus
two sessions

**TRAINEES**
Ones relatively
unfamiliar with
professional
terminology

# MAKING A TERMINOLOGY BOARD

## Preparation

1 At the same time as you give out a reading list, hand out a list of important terms that occur in the suggested reading.
2 Ask trainees to note down brief definitions of each term as they come across it in their reading. They can check their definitions with anyone they like.

## Procedure

1 In groups, trainees decide on a good definition for each term. They can confer with other groups and use dictionaries (see especially the *Dictionary of Linguistics and Phonetics* Crystal 1985)
2 While trainees are working on the definitions, lay out large sheets of cardboard, coloured felt tip pens, glue, sheets of stiff card, sellotape, staples, etc.
3 Trainees have ninety minutes to complete a 'terminology board'. (See instructions below, and Figure 9.) Explain that the group will have to decide: how the board is to be made, who will make it, who will make the definition cards, who will check the spelling, and so on.
   *Instructions:* Take a piece of thick card. Cut vertical slits into the card at regular intervals. The slits need to be 3–5 cm long. You'll need two slits for every pocket. Cut strips of thinner card for the terminology and definitions to be written on. These strips need to be cut so that they fit into the pockets. They can be glued, stapled and sellotaped for extra security.
4 If the boards are not quite finished at the end of the session, the groups present/explain their terminology boards in plenary at the beginning of the next session.
5 If some empty spaces are left on the boards, trainees add new terms met later in the course.

**VARIATIONS**
a The whole process can be done as a pre-course task, as in-course work or as review before an exam.
b All the groups can work with the same terms or each group can work with different terms from the others.
c The boards can be left up on the walls during the course so that terms can be reviewed and new terms added.

**RATIONALE/COMMENTS**
a The groups soon find out who has practical skills, such as an accurate eye for visual detail and nice handwriting, and where the intellectual strengths of the trainee group lie.
b The trainees work out for themselves the meanings of a whole series of professional terms.
c Motivation and a sense of achievement are very high with such an end product to work towards.

**d** Trainers have a valuable opportunity to watch the skills and personalities of the groups emerge and develop.

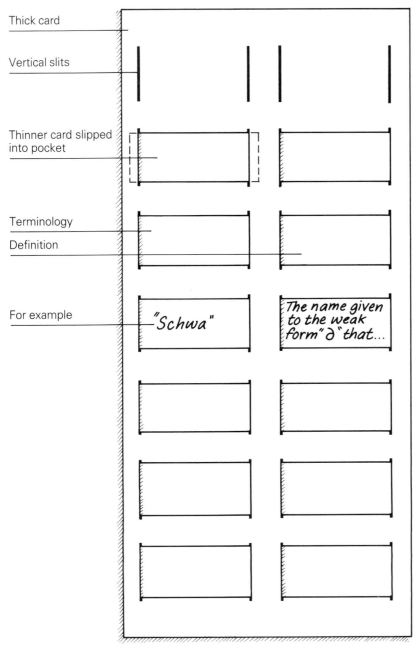

Thick card

Vertical slits

Thinner card slipped
into pocket

Terminology

Definition

For example

"Schwa"

The name given
to the weak
form" ∂ "that...

Fig. 9 A terminology board

ACKNOWLEDGEMENT/READING
I learnt this from Sara Walker (see Walker 1988) who got the idea of a
terminology board from Diana Fried-Booth (Fried-Booth 1986).

## 4.15

**MATERIALS**
One large empty cardboard box and plenty of blank cards

**TRAINEES**
Relatively inexperienced

# THE TERMINOLOGY POSTBOX
## Procedure

1 As professional terms come up during a course, write them on cards (or ask a trainee to) and put the cards in the 'postbox'. Example terms on the cards might be *competence, intonation, discourse* or any other specialised word or phrase that comes up during input of discussion.

2 At the end of a day, week, month or other part of the course, organise a team game. Teams take it in turns to pull out a card from the postbox. A member of the team whose turn it is has to define, explain or demonstrate the word(s) on the card. If this is done well, the team gets a point. Continue until all the cards are out of the box.

3 People who have bungled a word can take the card away with them to check the correct meaning. When they bring it back, it goes in the postbox again so that it is reviewed again next time.

**VARIATION**
Trainees can look through the contents of the box any time they wish to revise their understanding of terms or want to see if they've missed anything.

**RATIONALE/COMMENT**
Trainers have to be aware of what terms are new to trainees. Terminology is dealt with thoroughly and reviewed just as any other new material would be.

ACKNOWLEDGEMENT
I learnt this from Gillie Cunningham.

## 4.16

**MATERIALS**
None

**CONTENT**
Any that is visualisable (see below)

# ZANY VISUALISATIONS
## Procedure

1 As part of a review exercise, ask trainees to close their eyes and bring to mind the visual image suggested by the input you are reviewing. Examples of input that is visualisable are (1) finger correction – the use of the teacher's fingers to demonstrate contractions, syllable or word number, stress, etc., (2) board layout – the use of margins for new words that crop up unexpectedly in a lesson, etc., (3) monitoring groupwork – low profile, discreet monitoring versus more interventionist 'helping', etc.

2 Once trainees have a clear mental image of this ask them to make changes to the visual image in the way you suggest. Give time for the visual images to form clearly and then give instructions, with a long pause in between each, for the trainees to:
- 'Make the image pink.'
- 'Make it huge.'
- 'Make it tiny.'

- 'Make it disappear.'
- 'Bring the image back but . . . one hundred years ago.'
- 'Take the image to the year 3000.'
- 'Bring the image back to normal.'
- 'Add music to it.'

And so on.

3 If they like, they can discuss what they saw with a neighbour.

### RATIONALE/COMMENT

This activity, apart from being fun, encourages mental flexibility and can make certain types of material more memorable.

ACKNOWLEDGEMENT

I learnt this from Cynthia Beresford.

# CHAPTER 5

# *The teaching encounter*

A major part of most trainers' work is helping trainees to plan, prepare and observe lessons and watch trainees teach. Depending on your situation you will have your own normal ways of doing this. For example, it may be normal in your institution to give out a standard lesson plan format near the start of the course and to encourage trainees to stick to it as closely as possible.

In my institution on pre-service courses, observation is usually done with one trainer and four trainees watching small classes of non-paying language students who don't have to take any tests. Normal feedback for two Tunisian trainers I met once was writing up a report on observed English language teaching, in French, and reading it out to the teacher who had been observed in the presence of her boss and in her boss's office.

We all tend to feel that what we do is normal. But, thankfully, there are thousands of different norms. This chapter details a number of different ways that lesson planning, observing and feedback can be done. It attempts to share some of these different norms so that we can incorporate them, with adaptations, into our work.

Throughout the chapter there is mention of people (trainers or trainees) observing classes and giving feedback after 'teaching'. By this I don't just mean observation of and feedback on live lessons. I also include experiencing or learning about lessons via video or sound recording, TV or radio broadcasts, oral recapping by the teacher or an observer of a class, or by reading written lesson reports, lesson transcripts, lesson plans, teacher diaries or looking at pictures, diagrams and other visuals showing, for example, student interaction patterns.

In terms of lesson length, 'teaching' here is taken to include (a) whole lessons, and (b) 'micro' lessons, that is, lessons that are shorter in time or smaller in number of students (perhaps even one-to-one) or that contain less content, fewer steps or fewer objectives than a full lesson.

In terms of the type of language class involved, 'teaching' is here taken to include: lessons taught to classes of peers, one-off classes, borrowed classes, regular classes and specially made up classes taught by trainers, teachers, trainee teachers or a combination of these, with or without observers present. 'Teaching' also includes the work that a *trainer* does with trainees in what are often called 'input sessions'. Thus, training is a kind of teaching. 'Teaching' also includes mother tongue, foreign language or other subject lessons.

In this chapter, then, 'teaching' is taken to involve any combination of the variables of time, participant and so on mentioned above. Thus, to take some unusual combinations, it can involve language students watching a video of a class they have just attended, or trainees watching a trainer doing an input session, or trainees attending parallel language classes, or anyone recalling a learning experience from the past. This means that the work on lesson planning, observation and feedback can be adapted for use in any of these situations.

# Section 1: Working on lesson planning

This section deals with how to work on lesson plans. The assumptions are that lesson planning can be useful, that it can be learned gradually over a period of time and that basic plans can be developed into many different and creative types, with help from trainers, fellow trainees and students. The 'zero-option', no planning at all, is also mentioned.

One process idea that is not mentioned in this section is the simple giving out of lesson plan models, the format of which all trainees must follow every time they teach.

## 5.1

**MATERIALS**
Two large writing
surfaces, e.g. two
boards

**TRAINEES**
Pre-service, or any
who would like to
have practice
writing their own
lesson plans

# BASIC LESSON PLANS
## Procedure

1  Ask trainees to brainstorm onto the board the possible sub-headings a lesson plan might have. Step out of the way and watch. Figure 10 shows what one group of pre-service trainees came up with.

2  Have a good look at what trainees have written. Take what you can from it and organise it, with trainee help, into a skeleton lesson plan by using a second surface such as a flipchart or OHP. Thus, from the example brainstorm in Figure 10 you could take 'aim' and 'assumption' as lesson plan sub-headings. (There are other items in the array that you could take too.)

Aim  Practice  Exercise  Method  Presentation
Equipment  Register  Content  Different uses of  Recall
Assumptions  Vocabulary  language
Grammar  Feedback  Warm-up  Role play
Before the lesson  Pair/Groupwork  Known lexis
Materials required

Fig. 10 Brainstorm of lesson plan sub-headings

Iron out any problems that are implied by what is on the board. For example, 'role play'. Would you really do one *every* lesson? No? So is this a useful *general* heading?

3  After discussion, the trainees end up with a skeleton lesson plan. Here is a possible result:

Skeleton lesson plan

Teacher's name_____     Class_____

Date_____     Slot/Time_____

Information about the students:

Aim

Equipment

Known lexis and structures

Anticipated problems

Before the lesson

Methods or steps

What goes into the skeleton plan will depend upon what went up on the board, what you can take or adapt from that, plus other headings that you feel are really important. You can encourage trainees to check against the teacher's books that go with student coursebooks to see if there is anything useful in them that they've left out.

4 Next, indicate or elicit little starter phrases for each sub-heading, for example:

'Aim': 'By the end of the lesson the students should be able to . . .'; for 'Anticipated problems': 'Some students may find it difficult to . . .'

## RATIONALE/COMMENT

**a** Not all trainees will want or need to reinvent the wheel and write their own lesson plans from scratch. Some will, however, and it may take time for them to be able to do this. We don't usually expect trainees to teach excellent lessons right from the start. We are usually quite happy, the first couple of times, if trainees manage to hold the class's attention at important points and help the students to 'get through' a little material! It makes sense, then, to follow this attitude through into lesson planning, first being happy if *some* sort of plan or section of a plan is produced before the lessons are taught, and then gradually working on fuller, better plans in respect of format, degree of detail, and usefulness. Being content if people get things somewhat right and being happy with that amount of correctness is an attitude that, I feel, needs to be present in training as well as in teaching.

**b** The headings that are included in the brainstorm and lesson plan above betray a bias towards a particular type of language lesson, one where the teacher starts out with a language aim and throughout the lesson works towards it only. If you favour a different kind of language lesson within a method such as CLL (Counselling Language Learning; see Curran 1972 and 1976), this type of lesson plan will be irrelevant to you and you will want to think more in terms of follow-up and language research after the lesson than planning beforehand. But trainees could still find it useful to have a sheet bearing the main stages of a lesson within this method, with room for notes and reminders.

## 5.2

**MATERIALS**
None

**TRAINEES**
Ones wishing to
improve their
ability to write
their own lesson
plans

**NOTES**
This follows on
from 5.1 *Basic
lesson plans*

# BUILDING BETTER LESSON PLANS
## Procedure

Once trainees can regularly and reliably produce a skeleton lesson plan or part of a plan without too much help from you, you can help them to gradually improve their lesson plans by introducing the following improvements, one at a time. (These are not in order of importance.)

**a** For example, if, under 'Aim', trainees have been writing things like 'To teach the Present Perfect', get them thinking about which use, person (singular or plural), aspect (Simple or Progressive), whether affirmative, negative or interrogative, with or without tags, and so forth. Instead of 'Getting the phrases right', under 'Anticipated problems', work towards an understanding of the role of stress, intonation, contraction, spelling, collocation difficulties and so on.

**b** Add more headings

For example, add a 'Timing' column down the right-hand side of the page. Then, a bit later on, put in *two* timing columns, one for 'Estimated time', the other for 'Actual time'. Put in extra headings for other things you or the trainees or students think would be helpful.

**c** Collapsible, extendable sections

Ask trainees to mark with brackets or coloured pens what could be left out of their lessons if time is short and what could be put in or extended if things go more quickly during the lesson than anticipated. This kind of planning will eventually help teachers to think on their feet.

**d** Working documents

Encourage trainees to use larger sheets of paper, capitals, large lettering, 'neon' markers, colour, arrows and diagrams so that the plan becomes a useful working document that can be left on a desk and seen from a few feet away, rather than held with shaky hands and peered at.

**e** The student's point of view

Under the 'Steps' heading ask trainees to draw a vertical line down the middle of the page, forming two columns, as in Figure 11. Encourage trainees to write something in both columns for each step.

| STEPS | |
|---|---|
| **What teacher does** | **What students do** |
| 1 Give instructions for what Ss should do with text | Ss listen |
| 2 Check instructions are understood | Ss reply |
| 3 Hand out text | Ss receive |
| 4 Wait and be quiet | Ss read the text |

Fig. 11 Split lesson plan

**f** Zero-plan option

Can trainees react to students spontaneously when they meet them or do they have to glance at their lesson plans before saying 'hello'? Can the trainee teach a lesson *without* a plan? Does the trainee have some experience of lessons that hardly need a plan, for example, certain phases of CLL lessons? Has the trainee both talked to and observed experienced teachers who in their own words, 'Never plan'? The writing of hundreds of plans and objectives can sometimes lead to a concentration on the conspicuous, observable changes in language student performance and on the *teacher's* aims. It can lead to trainees forgetting that students are individuals with their own ideas and questions.

**g** Other people's plans

Make sure trainees have seen plenty of different style lesson plans created by other people (including peers on the course) as well as ones appearing in teacher's resource books, teacher's books linked to student coursebooks and teacher training manuals.

Have the trainees seen the plans *you* make before your input sessions? If you yourself do not make session plans, then the reasons are worth discussing in detail with your group.

**h** Different formats

Encourage trainees to change from a one or two page linear plan to other formats including hand-held filing cards (such as presenters use for lectures), mind maps, overlapping circles, pie-charts and lists of key words – until they find a format that is visually and organisationally satisfying to them. There may well be trainees who need to think through or mime through their sequences rather than write them down. Give time for this, then sit with the trainees while they describe, in their own way, what they will do.

**i** Addressing specific teaching practice problems

Encourage trainees to write onto the plan anything that will help them with a problem specific to them as an individual. So, for example, if a trainee forgets to ask concept questions, ask them to write some concept questions down in several places on the plan. If their instructions tend to be long-winded and unclear, ask them to work out better ones with a colleague and write them onto the plan in capitals or in a different colour.

**j** Plans for different types of lesson

Make sure trainees have attempted written plans for different types of lesson, for example, ones on grammar points, functions and exponents, vocabulary, discourse features, receptive and productive skills, topics or themes, cultural points, literature; ones that are task- or activity-based; ones with different phases (e.g. accuracy, fluency, teacher-centred presentation, student-centred work); ones of different length; solo and team-teaching lessons. Give them a chance to experience lessons where totally different sorts of 'planning' are required, for example, lessons to diagnose or review rather than teach, where students give presentations and so on.

**k** Plans written at different times

Check that trainees have written plans for their own lessons, for other people to teach from, and after watching someone else's lesson. A plan written after watching someone else teach can be written as in Figure 12.

| What happened | What could happen another time |
|---|---|
| 1 *T wrote up key words on board, e.g. birthday, Xmas, yesterday. Threw ball to Ss asking them to throw ball to someone else and ask that person a question using one of the key words.* | *Now Ss know the game, Ss can give their own key words. Or T can choose key words that work on different language area, e.g. tomorrow, after class, at the weekend, to practise, 'going to' future.* |

Fig. 12 What happened vs what could happen another time

**l** Lessons planned by language students

Encourage trainees to discuss with language students what they would like to learn in the next lesson, in what order, and how. Language students note down or dictate their lesson ideas for the trainee, who then teaches according to the learners' plan.

**m** Departing from plans

Have trainees had plenty of encouragement and practice in departing from plans when appropriate? Is there a heading on the plan called 'Thinking on my feet' that is filled in only after the lesson has been taught?

**n** Lesson plan sequences

Trainees need to have written a sequence of plans to show how items that come up can be reviewed, extended, consolidated and, if necessary, retaught.

**RATIONALE/COMMENT**

Once trainees can write a basic lesson plan, it is easy for them to 'plateau' at that level and for them to resent producing the same sort of work over and over again. *Building better lesson plans* shows concrete ways you can help trainees refine the detail of their planning and teaching.

# PLANNING THE TRAINER'S DEMONSTRATION

## Procedure

1 Tell the trainees you would like to teach them, for example, seven or eight words in a language they don't know. These words are a lexical set (for example, words for different kinds of fruit). Tell the trainees you would like these words to become part of their active vocabulary (for a while, at least). Ask them to discuss how they would like to be taught these words.

2 Divide the trainees into small groups for discussion and ask them to note down a detailed teaching procedure.

3 Monitor the groups and make sure that they consider all relevant issues, such as when they want to see the written form and how many times they want to hear a word before being asked to say it themselves.

4 Get members of different groups to exchange their ideas and then, with the whole class, draw up a consensus procedure on the board. Encourage discussion while this is going on.

5 Teach the vocabulary to the trainees using the procedure they themselves have provided. Follow their recipe *exactly*.

6 Discuss the procedure they suggested in the light of their experience of it as learners. The whole group makes any amendments they wish.

7 If you and the group wish, you can teach the lesson again as a kind of second draft. The same lexical set can be used but with different words or a different lexical set can be chosen.

**MATERIALS**
A large writing surface and, possibly, some visual aids (depending on the trainees' suggestions for a teaching procedure)

**TRAINEES**
Relatively inexperienced or pre-service

### VARIATIONS

a Trainees stipulate inclusion of particular micro-skills, for example, dialogue building or composition – depending on their ability in the foreign language.

b Trainees choose the aim of the lesson.

### RATIONALE/COMMENT

a Trainees are not dazzled by amazing techniques they have never thought of.

b The practice of planning in the abstract and then assessing and evaluating in the light of experience directly parallels the process of the trainees' own lesson planning and classroom contact. It's even neater, though, since there is also feedback and retrial!

c Trainees are reminded what it's like to be a language learner, and you are reminded what it's like to be a language teacher!

ACKNOWLEDGEMENT/READING
I got this idea from John Carmichael (see Carmichael 1987). See also Bolitho (1979) and Wajnryb (1990).

## 5.4

**MATERIALS**
See the different ideas

**TRAINEES**
Relatively inexperienced ones

# SOMETHING TO START PLANNING FROM
## Procedure

As a stage between (1) writing trainees' lesson plans for them, or (2) providing model plans to guide them in writing their own plans, and (3) trainees writing their own plans individually from scratch, here are some alternatives:

a Give trainees all the stages of a lesson plan but in jumbled order. They have to sequence the stages and rewrite the plan.

b Give them a lesson plan that looks like a recipe for chaos. They have to spot potential problems and improve the plan.

c Give them the main aim of a teaching slot and all the materials necessary for teaching the lesson a particular way. Materials could include a wallchart, tape, flashcards, dialogue grid, role-play cards, etc. They have to write a plan for the aim and steps that incorporate the materials.

d A group of trainees who are not teaching write a plan for someone who is.

### RATIONALE/COMMENT

'Help with plans' can prevent trainees feeling blocked when faced with a blank sheet of paper and being required to plan a lesson from scratch. It provides something for them to start with.

## 5.5

**MATERIALS**
See below

**TRAINEES**
Any who can write basic lesson plans

# DIFFERENT THINGS TO DO WITH LESSON PLANS
## Procedure

Once trainees can regularly write reasonably detailed lesson plans of various types for themselves and others, there are plenty of different things they can do with the plans. Here are some alternatives:

a Write lesson plans for trainees yourself. They teach the lessons. The plans contain materials, activities and/or steps new to them.

b Trainees write lesson plans for each other to teach. They then watch the lessons they planned being taught. The writers can see the advantages and disadvantages of their suggestions as they are not preoccupied with having to implement them themselves.

c Trainees write plans for you. This way, you are reminded how difficult it is to teach according to someone else's plan. You can also show the trainees what their own ideas are like in practice, or can enhance simple ideas in the classroom to show how they can be fully exploited or extended.

d Trainees observe a lesson and then write down what they think the teacher's aim was or what they think the main phases of the lesson were.

e Write the first half of a lesson plan. Ask trainees to complete it individually or in groups. Enjoy the differences.

**f** Write the last half of a lesson plan. Ask trainees to imagine or write what the first half could have been.

**g** If you have been teaching trainees the various steps of, for example, a presentation and controlled practice skills lesson, write down all the stages of the lesson. (See page 00 for the early stages of an inductive presentation.)

(1) Photocopy enough sheets to have one for each trainee. Then cut up each sheet into slips with one stage on each slip. (2) Put the slips into envelopes. (3) As trainees watch a lesson on, say, presentation and practice, they pull the slips out of their envelopes and try to match and sequence the steps they have with what they see.

This helps trainees to get organised and helps trainers to stay realistic about the fit between theoretical model stages and classroom practice.

**h** Give a lesson plan to trainees. They watch the lesson. While watching, they tick off the stages on the lesson plan as they recognise them. Alternatively, trainees write down the phrases used by the teacher to mark the different stages (e.g. 'Let's move on to look at some new words') or write down the seating arrangement for each stage.

**i** Show the trainees a seating diagram, as in Figure 13.

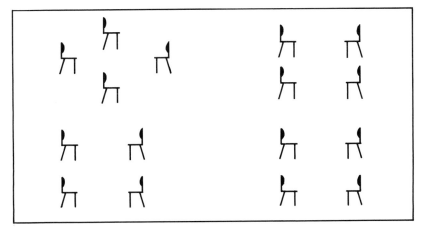

Fig. 13 Seating diagram

Trainees discuss what could be going on, what the teacher and students could be saying, why the chairs are in that arrangement, what might have happened beforehand, and what could be going to happen next. Then, trainees write a possible lesson plan to accompany a sequenced set of seating diagrams.

**j** Ask trainees to write three different kinds of lesson plan for their next three teaching slots.

For the first, they start from a piece of teaching material you give them such as a reading text.

For the second, they start with an aim they design themselves.

For the third, they start from a brief informal chat with students asking them what they would like to learn and do in the next lesson.

**RATIONALE/COMMENT**

This stage of working on lesson planning aims to encourage flexibility. By writing plans for others, filling in the first and last halves of other people's plans and experimenting with the order,

plan ⟶ teaching          teaching ⟶ plan and aim

teaching ⟶ plan          material and students ⟶ plan

trainees gain a more useful, knockabout, iconoclastic view of the lesson plan.

ACKNOWLEDGEMENT

Variation (h), 'observing and ticking' is an idea I got from Mike Harding.

---

## 5.6

**MATERIALS**
Some stimuli for conversation (see page 101)

**TRAINEES**
Trainees about to teach for the first time. This process works well with groups of trainees who are going to teach the same group of students

**REQUIREMENT**
A room with plenty of space for each group of trainees and their students. Ideally, each group of trainees should be twice as large as each group of language students

## THE FIRST TIME A *GROUP* OF TEACHERS TEACH

Pre-service trainees often get nervous about meeting language students for the first time. They may have memories of their own schooldays, memories of past teachers and past failures or worries about 'performing' at a time when they feel they don't know anything much about teaching.

We need ways of making first meetings between pre-service trainees and language students less nerve-racking and more human for all concerned. We need to be able to place first-time teachers in situations where they can listen to students, find out about them as human beings, find out their level, and get used to being in a classroom and coming out unscathed! Here is a selection of ways of doing this.

## Procedure

**PREPARING THE TRAINEES FOR MEETING THE STUDENTS**

1 Explain to trainees that the whole point of the first meeting is to meet the language students as fellow humans! Introduce them to a range of simple name-learning and warm-up exercises, preferably by doing them with the trainees.

2 Explain that when they and the students first meet, they can start off as a whole group, learning names and warming up, before dividing into threes (two trainees to one language student, or as near to this ratio as numbers will allow). This will involve moving some furniture.

3 Explain that, after the name-learning phase, in the two-to-one encounters, the idea is for one trainee to talk and listen to the language student they are with and for the other only to listen. No correction of students' language whatsoever is allowed. Since it can be hard to keep a conversation going by 'just chatting', introduce them to some simple stimuli for initiating conversations. (See 'Ideas for conversational stimuli' on page 101.)

## Ideas for conversational stimuli

a  The family tree (see 6.25 *Case Studies*)

One of the trainees starts by drawing a simple tree diagram of her family. The trainee explains to the language students who everyone is. Then, one student is encouraged to draw a similar tree and talk about her family in turn.

b  The sociogram (see 6.25 *Case studies*)

One of the trainees starts by drawing a sociogram with her name in the centre, with the names of close friends on the inner circles and less close friends on the outer rings. The trainee uses the diagram to talk briefly about these friends, where they live and why they are close friends. The student is then invited to draw a sociogram of her friends.

c  A plan of my room

One of the trainees draws a simple diagram of their bedroom or study and, while drawing, explains where things are, their shapes, colours and so on. The language student is then invited to draw a plan of the room she is staying in at the moment, or her room at home and describe it too.

d  Prepared questions

One of the trainees explains to the students that they both have a minute to write down five to ten interesting questions to ask. When they have done this, both ask the questions and let conversation develop from this.

4  Ask the trainees who are only going to listen to predict what sort of vocabulary, verb forms or set phrases could come up given the type of stimulus and what they know about the level of the group of students. The trainees write or type these items down the left side of a sheet of paper. Across the top they write students' names. This way they have a grid that will help them to take notes faster. In Figure 14 overleaf there is a specimen grid written for a conversation about a picture of a family dinner party taking place at night in a posh garden conservatory. Thus, we can see from this grid that the student was able to describe the picture using the present continuous tense but found speculation about what happened before or after the picture more difficult.

5  Once you have explained the first four steps and answered any queries, leave the trainees alone to organise themselves. To help them to do this, you can give them the task sheet on page 103.

### DURING THE ENCOUNTER (i.e. THE FIRST TEACHING PRACTICE)

6  You can join in the name-learning and warm-up activities and then withdraw to monitor each table for a while.

7  In the 'conversation' part, the same two trainees work together through the two-to-one phase of the getting acquainted/teaching practice slot, sticking to the same conversation stimulus. The room thus needs to be arranged for groups of three, perhaps with each threesome around a table, and with all the tables placed around the room café-style.

Name of language student....*Valeria*...............

| | Can do | Can't do |
|---|---|---|
| **Basic vocabulary** e.g. People, food, table, windows, light, etc. | *women, man, family, dinner, window* | *married couple, main course huge, airy, light* |
| **Higher vocabulary** e.g. Sweater, skirt, tomatoes, cauliflower, cutlery | *dress, suit, vegetables, tomatoes, knife* | *evening dress, skirt, cauliflower, mushroom, fork, spoon.* |
| **And higher** e.g. Matching napkins, reflection, window pane, bow tie, etc. | | |
| **Tenses e.g.** What are they doing? What did they do before they came to the party? | *✓ They're having dinner.* | *✗ They dress before they come.* |
| **Conditional** If it was daylight, what could you see outside? | *not attempted.* | |
| **Functional phrases** For congratulating thanking polite requests | *Here you are! ✓ Thanks a lot ✓ Can you ✓* | *✗ May you* |

Fig. 14 Example diagnostic grid

**8** One trainee will fill in the prepared grid with ticks or examples of what the student actually says, while the other keeps the conversation going.

**9** Trainees set a time limit after which the *language students* change tables and start new conversations with new trainees who, again, all use the same stimuli as they did before with their earlier students.

Example task sheet to help trainees with Step 5

You will need to decide:
- who greets the students and sets up and stops the first name-learning activity,
- who sets up and stops the warm-up activities you do after that,
- how many of these activities there will be,
- who explains the aim of the next phase,
- who reorganises the tables,
- who explains what to do,
- which trainees will work with which stimulus,
- which trainees will work together,
- who in each pair will be the initiator and who will prepare and use the grid,
- who will give the signal for language students to change tables,
- how many changes there will be,
- how long the warm-up phase will be,
- how long each conversation in the two-to-one phase will be,
- how long the two-to-one phase will be,
- who will draw the TP to a close, thank the students and ask them to come back next time.

© Longman Group UK Ltd 1992

**AFTER THE ENCOUNTER**

**10** Leave the trainees to hold their own feedback for a while around the concerns which you suggest to them on the discussion sheet. (See the example below).

Example discussion sheet for Step 10

- What have we learned about each student's name, background, likes and dislikes and so on?
- What was the proportion of teacher talking time to student talking time?
- What have we discovered about what individual students can or can't handle linguistically?
- Does this give us any idea of what the students might need/like to learn in the future TP slots?
- How difficult was it to concentrate on language rather than on communicative content?
- Were there any advantages (in terms of eye contact, relaxation, etc.) to having a stimulus rather than just chatting?

© Longman Group UK Ltd 1992

**11** You can join in at some stage towards the end of the discussion and can:

- show trainees what one of the conversation ideas looks like written up in a 'recipe' format in a book. For example, show them the sociogram idea as it appears in *Grammar in Action* (Frank and Rinvolucri 1983 p. 68),
- discuss the differences in language that might have come up in the different activities,
- discuss any observations on 'teacheritis', for example, a teacher distorting the naturalness of language by slowing down, shouting, oversimplifying or introducing verbal tics,
- discuss any hitches in class management or in timing.

### RATIONALE/COMMENT

**a** Trainees work in pairs and so feel supported.

**b** They get to grips with one activity and the language it is likely to throw up.

**c** They plan the whole TP session as a group.

**d** Students and trainees get to know each other as individuals.

**e** Trainees are not required to teach students a language point before meeting them as human beings or seeing what they need.

**f** Later teaching points can be based around the student needs noticed in this first session.

## 5.7

### MATERIALS
Some stimuli for conversation (as for 5.6, see page 101)

### TRAINEES
Ones who are about to teach for the first time but who are not going to share a class with a group of trainees on the same course

## THE FIRST TIME AN *INDIVIDUAL* TEACHER TEACHES
## Preparation

**1** Read 5.6 *The first time a group of teachers teach.*

**2** If the language students know each other well, trainees skip part of the ice-breaker phase. For rooms absolutely packed with people and furniture, moving around is more trouble than it's worth. For first-time teachers working by themselves with large groups of students, there is no friend to help monitor student language and no colleague to take over and organise different phases of the lesson, so you will need to select carefully from the ideas for conversational stimuli (5.6 page 101).

### VARIATIONS

**a** Language students write down, in class, ten questions each that they would like to ask the first-time teacher. The teacher strolls around reading and helping with the questions and then sits, listens and answers as students ask them out loud.

**b** Students, in pairs or threes, work with key words or pictures to compose as many sentences as they can in a time limit. Students then read out their sentences. Other students judge the sentences as correct/incorrect, interesting/boring, true/false. Points are awarded accordingly. The first-time teacher, who can have prepared a language grid (see 5.6, Fig. 14) for the key words or for the pictures, makes notes about student abilities as the students speak.

**c** Students prepare five true statements about their neighbour, check these with their neighbour and then introduce their neighbour to the teacher.

**d** Students draw plans of anything the first-time teacher needs to know, for example, the position of toilets, stairs, fire exits, canteen, staff-room, nearest bus stop, and so on. One student comes to the board to start drawing a plan of the school. Other students call out suggestions and explanations in answer to the teacher's queries, such as, 'Where can I get something to drink?' 'How do I get to town?' 'Where is the head teacher's office?'

### RATIONALE/COMMENT

**a** Trainees are not required to teach students a language point before meeting them as human beings and also seeing what they need.

**b** Later teaching points can be based around the student needs noticed in this first session.

**c** Even if these activities are only used for five or ten minutes of the first lesson a teacher teaches, besides enabling the teacher and students to meet as human beings, they help the teacher to be low-profile, and give students something to say and the teacher something to listen to.


# Section 2: Preparing for observation

This section aims to help those – whether trainees or trainers – who are about to be observed or who are about to observe someone else teach or train. It deals with the issues of courtesy, viewpoint and first impressions, as well as with the difficulties of deciding what to see, how to record it and how to weigh its significance. It does not cover the practice of arriving at a teacher's door unannounced and expecting to be let in!


## COULD YOU BE MY TEACHER?

## Procedure

1 Ask trainees to think of something that they would like to learn, for example, how to walk on their hands, do calculus, weave, deliver jokes effectively, and so on.

2 They move into pairs. One person is A, the other is B. Everyone keeps their letter designation for the rest of the activity.

**5.8**

**MATERIALS**
None

**TRAINEES**
Any

**3** A explains to B what she would like to learn and why. She also explains *how* she would like to learn it. She specifies the environment, time of day, the frequency of attempts, the type of teacher she'd like, and so on. B just listens.

**4** B says whether and to what extent she thinks she could meet the conditions A requires. A and B discuss whether B would make a good teacher for A in some or any respects.

**5** The pairs split up and people form new A–B pairs.

**6** This time the Bs say what they would like to learn and how. The As listen and then say if they think they'd make a good teacher for B.

### VARIATION

Trainees stay in the same pairs throughout the activity.

### RATIONALE/COMMENT

**a** By talking about their own learning preferences people become more aware of how normal classrooms cater for *groups* rather than for individuals, and of how different, and definite, people can be in their aims and preferences.

**b** It is openly recognised that any one teacher is not going to be right for everyone.

## 5.9

**MATERIALS**
A board or flipchart

**TRAINEES**
Any

# THE PERFECT OBSERVER

## Procedure

**1** Initiate a group discussion of times when people *watch* other people (e.g. at football matches, on underground trains, in restaurants when others are talking very loudly, and so on). Discuss how it feels to watch and to be watched.

**2** Invite people, in small groups, to say how they feel (or think they will feel) about having observers in their classrooms and to come up with a list of ten things they think would make The Perfect Observer both from their own and from the language students' point of view.

**3** Ask the groups to read out their 'top ten' lists and make a central list on the board. Refine the list as you go, to make sure there are no duplications. Allow plenty of discussion.

**4** Jot down a copy of the list for duplication and distribution or give all those who will observe or be observed time to write down their own copies.

### RATIONALE/COMMENT

**a** The initial discussion allows people to make public the normal fears and inhibitions concerned with 'performance'.

**b** The composite list-making in plenary encourages full discussion of the courtesies and practicalities involved in observing others at work.

# FIRST IMPRESSIONS – YOUR VOICE, YOUR LOOK

## Procedure

1 Play participants a tape of someone talking or singing. It helps if the voice is rather distinctive in some way and if the tape is about a minute long.
2 Ask people to guess the sex, age, nationality, height, weight, colouring, occupation and lifestyle of the speaker.
3 Next, show the participants a picture of a person and ask them to guess the same sorts of details about this person.
4 Discuss how strong our guesses, hunches and predictions can be about a person before we have even met them.
5 Discuss how these impressions might affect us when we are observing, being observed, learning or being taught.

**VARIATIONS**
To change this idea for use as a warm-up at the start of a course, ask participants to talk to each other about how they travelled to the course. They should divulge as little as possible about basic facts of their marital status, age, lifestyle and so on. After their talk about how they got there, trainees return to their seats and write down their speculations about their partner's biographical facts and lifestyle. Discussion follows.

**RATIONALE/COMMENT**
Students, teachers and colleagues may form strong impressions of each other which have nothing very much to do with actual performance and personality, but rather more to do with appreciation or dislike of someone's look, smell, mood, gait, voice or clothes. It's useful to remember this, since these impressions can be very strong and may affect the way we feel about people long after we start to know them and their work.

ACKNOWLEDGEMENTS
I experienced this activity first as part of a warm-up (led by Elayne Phillips) at the start of a course for teacher trainers. I learnt the variation from Gerlinde Wilberg.

**5.10**

**MATERIALS**
A tape of a distinctive voice talking or singing, a picture of an interesting looking person

**TRAINEES**
Any

# PAIR TEACHING

## Procedure

1 Trainees pair off. They decide what they can teach each other, for example, a bit of a foreign language, some tips on doing crosswords, juggling, etc.
2 First, A teaches B something.
3 Next, B gives feedback on what it was like to experience A's teaching. A listens very hard and takes notes if she wishes.

**5.11**

**MATERIALS**
Depends on what the teacher teaches

**TRAINEES**
Any

4 A repeats, as nearly word-for-word as possible, what B said as feedback.

5 A and B reverse roles and do the activity again.

6 Bring the whole group together and invite comment.

### VARIATIONS

a Participants declare at the start, to the whole group, what they feel they can offer to teach others. The pairing is done this time on the basis of who would like to learn what.

b Once A has taught B, B has given feedback and A has repeated it, participants change pairs and repeat the activity.

### RATIONALE/COMMENT

a This activity reminds trainees that they actually know a lot about teaching even though they may be feeling that they don't know much. The activity lets trainees see a different side of each other.

b After the phase of teaching, both sides get feedback. A gets some on her teaching and B on her feedback. This reminds trainees that they have a right to think about the quality and effect of feedback they get on the course.

c It is interesting to see how much of the feedback the teacher remembers. Individuals who find that they can't remember very much, or remember inaccurately, might want to make notes or check their understanding in future feedback sessions.

d This kind of micro-teaching is not 'hollow', not about things that people already know. It involves real, new content.

## 5.12

**MATERIALS**
None

**TRAINEES**
Any

**NUMBER OF SESSIONS**
Two, with project work in between

## PAIR PRACTICE OBSERVATION

## Procedure

### BEFORE THE OBSERVATIONS

1 They trainees pair up.

2 They choose to observe, at a time convenient to them, people doing any of the following activities: queueing, eating, making or taking phone calls, coming in and out of doorways (e.g. at the entrance to a shop or bank), greeting people they don't know (e.g. waiters, bar staff, bus conductors) or do know (e.g. classmates, family members at airports and railway stations), or any other activity that is easily observable in day-to-day circumstances.

3 The pair of observers have a talk beforehand to decide which activity they will watch (where and for how long) and to discuss a range of details that could be looked for, for example, gesture, facial expression, body movement, eye contact, language, and distance between participants.

4 The observers go off and do their observing.

**AFTER THE OBSERVATIONS**

**5** The pairs do any of the following:

    **a** They discuss with each other what they saw.

    **b** If both have made their own notes on what they observed, they read their notes aloud to each other and discuss similarities and differences in their observations.

    **c** They tell a third party what they saw *without* discussing it first with each other.

**RATIONALE/COMMENT**

    **a** The watching, recording and recapping involved here gives trainees a chance to be the observers and to experience the difficulties, delights and skills of observing.

    **b** Whichever way the pairs report back after their observation, there is likely to be some discussion of: what was expected; how their observations were the same or different; how easy or difficult it was to observe and record and what the significance was of what they saw.

ACKNOWLEDGEMENT

I learnt this from John Morgan.

# Section 3: During observations

In devising the ideas in this section I mostly had in mind trainees who have the chance to observe language classes taught by:

- each other,
- other teachers
- trainers

However, many of the ideas can be applied to:

- trainees/trainers listening to a tape or watching a video of one of their own or someone else's language classes or training sessions,
- observation by trainees of a trainer's input sessions,
- observation by trainers and teachers of other teaching events such as parallel language classes,
- use by teachers of records of teaching events such as lesson transcripts.

The aim is to develop and refine their ability to see and hear what goes on in a classroom by (1) looking for, and at, different elements of classroom action and (2) taking advantage of different ways of keeping observation records.

## 5.13

**MATERIALS**
Depends on the variation chosen

**TRAINEES**
Trainees who choose this method of observation

# 'DUAL CONTROL'; THE 'DRIVING INSTRUCTOR' MODEL

## Procedure

1 Ask trainees whether they would like help *during* their lessons. If the answer is 'yes', arrange with each trainee the times when intervention is acceptable and the type of intervention the trainee would prefer.

Convenient times may be: 'only if there's a real disaster going on', 'only when I'm monitoring groupwork', 'anytime when I'm not speaking' or 'anytime after the first few minutes'.

Types of intervention may be: holding up cards with words and symbols on, calling out one word or a short phrase (with a pleasant intonation), passing a written note, making pre-arranged gestures, or passing a signal via a radio transmitter (see reference for RAP below).

If a trainee says she would *not* like you to intervene, do not intervene in any way.

2 If a trainee has agreed times and types of intervention, then carry these out. For example, if you have agreed with a trainee to intervene if she seems not to have heard a student's remark, then intervene when this happens by, for example, pointing at the student (if you can be seen by the trainee but not the student), by turning to look at the student (if you are seated with the class) or by saying simply, 'Student', and looking at the student whose remark went unheard.

3 If at any time the teacher looks irritated or harrassed by your interventions, *stop* intervening.

4 Note carefully what happens after intervention. Does the trainee incorporate the intervention smoothly or look ruffled? The next time the situation comes up, does the trainee act differently? How do the language students react?

5 During feedback, check how the intervention procedures worked from the trainee's point of view and adjust them accordingly. Take care to note the language students' reactions too, and take time to talk to the students and with the trainee about what's going on. It's important to get the style and timing right for all concerned.

### VARIATIONS

a Fellow trainees help with interventions.

b Ask trainees to vote for more help with lesson planning, more help during classes or more help after (via feedback).

### RATINALE/COMMENT

a Some trainees feel that help before a lesson is too abstract and help afterwards is too late. Help during teaching suits those who want to have the experience of getting certain sequences right or making certain decisions while actually teaching.

b Variation (a) keeps peers on their toes.

ACKNOWLEDGEMENT
'Radio Assisted Practice Project' (RAP) (Tomlinson 1988).

## STRESS SIGNALS
### Procedure

1 Discuss with trainees what symptoms they might see in a person who is stressed, fearful or anxious in a classroom. Come up with a list of symptoms, for example, flushed face, sighing, nervous giggling, shallow breathing, and inability to make eye contact.
2 Ask trainees to watch for signs of stress in learners and teachers and to note them down during the next observation.
3 During feedback, invite trainees to mention any stress signals they noted in their students. They will probably be able to add to the list of symptoms at this stage.
4 Observations on teachers' stress symptoms need not necessarily be talked about openly in the group. Raising the topic in this way, though, often leads trainees to mention that they felt a bit stressed, harrassed or worried at some stage. This can then be discussed if it might help the trainee.

### EXTENSION

5 Work can be done on noting culture, age or gender-related differences in stress symptoms. For example, giggling or putting your head down can be a sign of quite severe stress in some cultures.

### RATIONALE/COMMENT

The process of detailed observation is applied here to the unusual area of stress. This can open up a discussion of the possible stressful nature of teaching and learning and of ways of making classes more enjoyable, less tense and, perhaps, less 'performance' based.

ACKNOWLEDGEMENT
Thanks to Mike Harding for alerting me to stress!

### 5.14
**MATERIALS**
None

**TRAINEES**
Any

## DEMONSTRATING IT ALL WRONG

### Procedure

1 Give a little demonstration (using trainees as a language class) of any aspect of language teaching that has come up on the course so far. For example, elicitation and teaching of vocabulary. The demonstration should include *lots* of things that are done wrongly (according to the gospel of the course or mainstream views in general).

### 5.15
**MATERIALS**
None

**TRAINEES**
Any

**2** Ask all trainees to act like language students except when they see you doing something they consider wrong. They then shout, 'Wrong!', For example:

| | |
|---|---|
| Trainer in the role of language teacher | Now I'm going to teach you forty difficult new words today. |
| Trainees acting as language students | Oh dear. |
| Trainees who have spotted something wrong | Wrong! |
| Trainer | Why? |
| Trainee 1 | Don't tell us they're difficult, it will discourage us! |
| Trainee 2 | How do you know they're all new to us? We might know some of them! |
| Trainee 3 | Forty is too many. |
| Trainer | Oh, OK. I'll start again. Does anybody know the word *giraffe?* |
| Some trainees | Yes. |
| Other trainees | No. |
| Another trainee | Wrong! Don't give us the word. Give us a clue and see if we can recall it! |
| Trainer | Right! Er, does anybody know the name of an animal? |
| Trainee 1 | Yes, a slug. |
| Trainee 2 | Wrong! Bad clue! etc. |

**3** (Optional) A scribe can be noting down all the things you do wrong. This list of misdemeanors can be read out later or photocopied and discussed.

**RATIONALE/COMMENT**

**a** Trainees get to tell you you're wrong.

**b** Trainers don't have to do 'perfect' demonstrations.

**c** You can do all the things you have noticed trainees doing in their teaching (practice), but reenacting these things yourself obviates the need for direct personal comments.

## 5.16

**MATERIALS**
A lesson plan

**TRAINEES**
Any

# REALITY COMPARED WITH THE LESSON PLAN
## Procedure

**1** Before an observed lesson, give the observer(s) a lesson plan that relates in some way to the lesson to be observed.

**2** While the lesson is being taught, the observer watches the lesson and works with the lesson plan in one of the following ways:

    **a** If given a lesson plan that has been cut into strips and jumbled up, she sequences the lesson plan according to how the lesson develops.

**b** If given a lesson plan with extra stages on it (i.e. stages that will not come up in the lesson to be taught), the task is to tick only the stages that happen.

**c** Given a plan with only an aim and broad headings, she fills in the detail of the stages as they occur.

**d** If given a lesson plan with steps written down the left of the page, the task is to fill in the apparent reasons for each step on the right side of the page. Alternatively, the right-hand side can be used to note down timing or to draw diagrams of where students and teacher are.

**3** The observers' work can be used in feedback to remind people of what actually happened in the observed lesson before people start to comment on the lesson.

### VARIATIONS

**a** Before the lesson, the observers receive only the lesson aim or the teaching point. They write a lesson plan to express how *they* would achieve the aim. When they observe the lesson, they note down differences between their own lesson plan and what actually occurs in the lesson.

**b** Before the lesson, observers receive a list of activities that the students are to do. From this, they try to predict in detail what vocabulary, tenses, functional phrases and so on will come up. They write these down the left side of a page. During the lesson, some observers tick off the language that was predicted and actually came up, other observers note down language that came up that was *not* predicted.

### RATIONALE/COMMENT

Playing about with stages, aims, reasons and bits of a lesson plan can help trainees to gain confidence and flexibility with them. This sort of work discourages a perfection-oriented, 'tablet of stone' approach to lesson plans and lessons.

## 5.17

**MATERIALS**
None

**TRAINEES**
Any

# STUDENT CONCENTRATION GRAPHS
## Procedure

**1** Trainees discuss how they think different people appear and behave if they are concentrating hard on a lesson. Elicit many different ideas, e.g. closing eyes, doodling, writing fast, etc.

**2** Ask observers to draw a simple graph as in Figure 15.

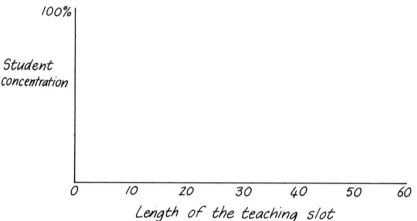

Fig. 15 Student concentration graph

**3** As they watch other people's lessons, they concentrate on a particular student. They need to sit somewhere where they can watch the student easily but not too obviously. They mark on the graph, using a simple wavy line, the degree of concentration apparently being shown by the student as the lesson progresses. At particular peaks and troughs they write down notes that explain what behaviour they have seen and any possible explanations for the degree of apparent concentration at that time.

A partly finished graph might look like Figure 16.

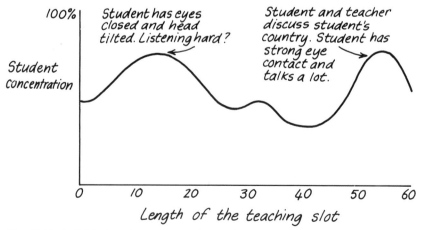

Fig. 16 Partly finished student concentration graph

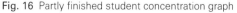

**4** In the feedback session, the graph(s) can simply be displayed or shown to the teacher, who may want to comment. Alternatively, teacher and observer(s) comment on the lesson and all look at the graphs to see what they show. A discussion can ensue on whether it is possible to tell when someone is concentrating, whether students should always be concentrating on other people (i.e. their teacher and their classmates) or whether they need reflection time, and so on.

### VARIATIONS

Observers produce graphs during different lessons or part lessons (i.e. during guided fantasies, story-telling/listening, mumbling exercises, counselling learning. . .) so that there is no assumption that one particular type of concentration alone is desirable.

### RATIONALE/COMMENT

**a** The process of detailed observation and record-making applied to students rather than teachers can help to get observers' attention off teacher performance and onto the students.

**b** It can also help to open up discussion on active students who are fun but seem to learn little, and on quiet students who learn a lot, as well as on cultural and personal differences in concentration patterns and study styles.

READING
Woodward (1989a).

## STUDENT INTERACTION DIAGRAMS
## Procedure

### 5.18

**MATERIALS**
Pen and paper

**TRAINEES**
Any

**1** The observer draws a seating plan with the names of students written on or, if there are very many students or their names are not all known, leaves the names off. See Figure 17.

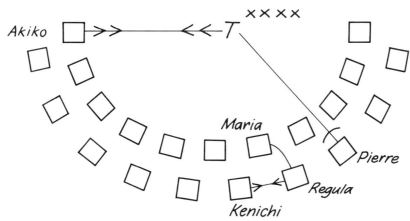

Fig. 17 Student seating plan

**2** As the lesson progresses, the observer indicates different kinds of interaction between students and the teacher by using different types of lines and symbols on the seating plan which they have drawn (see Figure 18).

**3** It is as well for observers to concentrate on just one type of interaction to start with, and only for, say, a ten-minute slot of the lesson, as this work is quite intense. Once observers can mark one type of interaction, they can start working with more than one type and for a longer time.

**4** After the lesson, observer(s) show(s) the diagrams to the person who taught. Anyone may ask questions or comment.

### VARIATIONS

**a** It is useful to mark who the teacher tends to look at in order to find out if she has a 'blind spot' or a 'hot spot'.

**b** Use other symbols for other types of interaction.

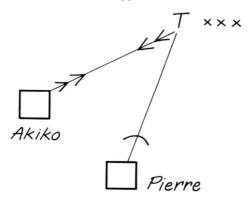

Fig. 18 Student seating plan showing teacher: student interaction

### GLOSSARY OF SYMBOLS

– Teacher asks questions and nominates a particular student: ⟶
 Each **>** stands for one question (see Teacher to Akiko).
– Teacher asks open question to whole class such as, 'Does anyone know . . .?': placement of an **✕** near T.
– Student responds to a teacher-initiated exchange: ⟶
 (see Akiko to Teacher).
– Student volunteers a remark without being prompted: ⟶)–
 (see Pierre to Teacher).

### RATIONALE/COMMENT

**a** The process of observing and coding information about interactions helps to get observers' attention off the teacher and onto classroom talk among all the participants.

**b** These diagrams are visual data that can be handed to someone who has taught in order to encourage discussion and reflection. The observer does not actually have to *tell* the person who has taught about a particular interaction habit. The diagrams provide a visual focus to feedback which balances the normal 'listen and talk' mode.

READING
Woodward (1989a).

# MOTHER TONGUE UTTERANCES
## Procedure

1  The observer sits near a student, a pair of students or a group of students during oral practice.
2  While the students are speaking, the observer either tape records or writes down verbatim all or part of what the students say in their mother tongue.
3  After observing, the observer works out, with help if necessary, the target language equivalents of the mother tongue utterances and notes them down.
4  The observer shows these notes to the teacher. The teacher may wish to comment on whether these potential target words and phrases have been presented to students or not. The teacher now knows what language *really* needs to be presented, practised or reviewed by students.

### RATIONALE/COMMENT
This dictation activity brings home to teachers the implications of doing pair or groupwork. It can encourage a natural syllabus, based on *real* student need in situations the teacher has thrown the students into. It can thus take some of the strain out of weekly planning by providing ideas for course content.

**5.19**

**MATERIALS**
Optional, a cassette recorder and blank cassette for each observer

**TRAINEES**
Any, but works best with trainees who know quite a lot of the students' mother tongue

# OBSERVING ASPECTS OF STUDENT TALK
## Procedure

1  The observer decides to watch one student or one group of students, possibly a group who all speak the same mother tongue, and sits where she can do this easily and unobtrusively.
2  The observer decides which aspects of student talk to make notes on, for example:
   ● the number of times a student speaks in a lesson,
   ● the number of times the student *initiates* an exchange,
   ● examples of correct language used by the student,
   ● examples of 'unEnglish' stress patterns,

**5.20**

**MATERIALS**
None

**TRAINEES**
Any

- examples of communication strategies the student uses when she doesn't know a word or phrase,
- examples of meaningful versus meaningless language.

3 The observer listens and makes notes on this so that she can share this information with the teacher after the lesson. The teacher may comment or ask questions.

4 The information can be shared with students too.

**RATIONALE/COMMENT**

a Both inexperienced and experienced teachers can be so concerned with their own performance that they cannot seem to hear, listen to, or really respond to what students say. The process of listening to, classifying and recording student utterances gives the observers valuable information about what was going on in a lesson from the students' point of view. The teachers are, in my experience, amazed at what they simply did not hear when they were 'busy teaching'.

b This process encourages trainees to use the data of the classroom as a basis for information and decision making.

## 5.21

**MATERIALS**
Observation sheet
(see below)

**TRAINEES**
Any

# OBSERVING ASPECTS OF TEACHER TALK
## Procedure

1 With the cooperation of the teacher, the observer decides what aspect of teacher talk to focus on.

2 During the lesson, the observer writes down *verbatim* any of the following:
- what the teacher says immediately after a student has spoken, as well as a bit of what the teacher has responded to,
- the ways the teacher praises students verbally,
- examples of teacher instruction language that is well over the heads of the students,
- good instructions,
- instances of meaningless language (i.e. language without a real communicative purpose, said only for practice purposes) or meaningful language,
- examples of slow, stilted or unnatural talk by the teacher.

Alternatively, rather than writing down a verbatim record the observer simply counts by ticking, for example, the number of times the teacher repeats what students say, uses the same boundary marker (e.g. 'OK. Right. Now then . . .'), reacts genuinely to a student contribution, or is silent and listens for longer than a split second.

(Observers may find it easier to listen and take notes if facing *away* from the class).

Figure 19 shows an example of part of a sheet for guiding an observer in noting instructions used by the teacher.

Instruction language observation sheet:

Teacher_____

Observer_____

Date_____ Time_____ Slot_____

Class level *Elementary*_____

Instructions:

In the boxes marked 'A' below, write verbatim examples of over-complex instruction language used by the teacher. Before you show this sheet to the teacher, try to rephrase this language into something more likely to be understood by these students. Write your rephrasing in the boxes marked 'B'. The first two boxes show examples:

A *"Now in retrospect, I'd like you to consider what you would have done had you been in Ned's shoes."*
*(Elementary!?)*

B *"Now, think!" (gesture) "You are Ned". (gesture)*
*"What can you do ?" (gesture)*

A

B

etc.

**Fig. 19** Instruction language observation sheet

**3** After the lesson, the observer gives the sheet to the teacher without comment. The teacher may want to ask questions or comment. The observer can do some work on the notes before showing them to the teacher, for example, rephrasing metalanguage or instructions or by suggesting additional expressions of praise if these have been a bit limited or repetitive in the lesson.

**VARIATION**

Teachers record one of their own lessons on audio-cassette. After the lesson they transcribe bits of it, and do the analysis above for themselves.

**RATIONALE/COMMENT**

**a** This training process of taking dictation/counting and recording focuses attention on teacher language rather than student language. Short verbatim examples, if written down faithfully, can act as real data in an otherwise rather impressionistic discussion of 'what I did' and 'what I think I saw and heard'.

**b** Asking the observer to do some work on the language they record encourages peer support.

ACKNOWLEDGEMENT/READING
For more detailed, thorough and complex observation schedules, see Allwright (1988).

## 5.22

**MATERIALS**
Observation sheet
(see below)

**TRAINEES**
Any

# ERROR CORRECTION STRATEGIES SHEET

## Procedure

1 Ask observers to concentrate on two things while they are observing: (a) incorrect student language, and (b) what the teacher does about it.
2 Ask them to use a sheet such as the example below.
3 As observers get quicker at using this sheet, a third column can be added ('What happened next') or a fourth ('Alternative methods'), which they fill in after the lesson.
4 After the lesson, encourage discussion of the language data and what it says about the students, about the correction strategy chosen and whether it was effective, and about alternative strategies.

**RATIONALE/COMMENT**
The error correction strategies sheet shown here is good for helping observers to listen to students, to distinguish between what is correct or not, and to notice the detail of a variety of correction strategies.

Error correction strategies sheet

Teacher_____   Observer_____
Date_____   Time_____   Slot_____
Level_____

Below, in the left-hand column, write down any incorrect student utterances. In the right-hand column, make notes on what the teacher did about them. The possibilities are: (1) consciously ignored, (2) didn't seem to hear, (3) asked student to repeat, (4) corrected with teacher voice, (5) corrected with gesture, (6) asked student to correct self, (7) asked named other student to correct, (8) asked whole class to help, (9) went to the board to draw/write something, (10) referred student to past example in text, on board or taped dialogue, (11) teacher repeated the whole thing with question intonation, (12) teacher repeated up to word before mistake, (13) other. You may find it easier to use numbers instead of writing notes in the right-hand column.

| Student mistake | Teacher action |
|---|---|
| e.g. 'she go there' | e.g. (4) T hisses 's' |

© Longman Group UK Ltd 1992

# QUESTIONS TO THE TEACHER
## Procedure

1 Give each observer an observation sheet (see Figure 20).
2 Using the sheet below during the observed lesson, the observer writes down any questions she would like to put to the teacher.
3 After the lesson, the observer gives the sheet to the teacher who then fills in the comments sections before feedback.
4 During feedback the sheet can be referred to overtly or it can simply be background to the conversation.

**5.23**

**MATERIALS**
Observation sheet
(see below)

**TRAINEES**
Any

---

Questions to the teacher
observation sheet

| Person watching | Person teaching | Date | Learner level |
|---|---|---|---|
| S.D. | H. | 14/7/91 | *Intermediates "Studying Strategies"* |

Person watching. As you watch, write any questions or comments that you'd like to put to the teacher. These can be related to the things you like, can't understand, have other ideas for, etc.

Question/Comment *Are they compatible? Can you think of a better seating arrangement?*

Answer *Sam couldn't see the board. It would have been better to operate the tape recorder outside the group or they could have sat on the chairs.*

Question/Comment *Who explained "bachelor"? Who could have?*

Answer *I did! I could have got an explanation from the group. More practice for them!*

Question/Comment *Your presence is so soothing to the group. Lovely today. Will it lead to a low-key feel overall or can you vary it when you need to?*

Answer *Yes, I'm sure. Movement - change of activity. Louder voice.*

Question/Comment *What ideas do you have for a follow-up, next lesson?*

Answer *I thought I'd get them to retell their stories to the other groups if they're still interested. What do you think?*

Question/Comment

Answer

Any other comments

Fig. 20 Questions to the teacher observation sheet

**VARIATIONS**

The question-and-answer format can be expanded to a letter written to the teacher by the observer during the lesson. The letter can include questions, notes on student reactions or the observer's reactions, sketches of boardwork and so on.

**RATIONALE/COMMENT**

This process of informal written conversation encourages a tentative approach by the observer rather than a judgmental one. It can encourage a natural expression of comment and curiosity.

ACKNOWLEDGEMENT/READING

I learnt this idea from Sheelagh Deller. See Deller (1987).

## 5.24

**MATERIALS**
Observation sheet
(see below)

**TRAINEES**
Any

# LITTLE BOXES BALANCE SHEET
## Procedure

Use a sheet like the one in Figure 21, which has been partly filled in to demonstrate its use. One by one, observers fill in the central boxes with brief descriptions of each of the steps in the teacher's lesson (e.g. 'T gave out picture'). They add comments to the left or right according to whether they spot an advantage or disadvantage to what is happening. They write any longer comments or questions horizontally between the boxes (e.g. 'Ss may be getting used to this by now . . .').

If both observer and teacher would like an (inexpensive) copy of the completed sheets, the observer uses carbon paper to make two copies of her comments and then gives both to the teacher, who in turn uses carbon paper to enter her comments on both sheets, one of which she can return to the observer.

| Things that seemed to work well | What you did | Points to consider |
|---|---|---|
| v. clear instructions | T elicited a letter from Ss + wrote it on board. Elicited 3 words starting with the letter. Ss in pairs. Fast talk on 3 topics. | José couldn't see the board |
| Brisk pace | | |

The Ss may be getting used to this now. They've done it 3 times. Let's discuss what this warm-up is for + what others could be used to achieve same aim.

T gave out picture.

Fig. 21 Little boxes balance sheet

**RATIONALE/COMMENT**

**a** The sheet can be filled in swiftly and in an organised way.

**b** Fairly objective notes are separated from subjective comments.

**c** It encourages a balance between negative and positive comments.

**d** Teachers can see at a glance what the observer saw them do in a lesson by reading down the central boxes. This aids fast recall of steps.

ACKNOWLEDGEMENT/READING

I learnt this from Lynn Rushton who learnt it from Tony Hopwood. See Rushton (1987).


# THE ALTERNATIVES OBSERVATION SHEET

## Procedure

**5.25**

**MATERIALS**
Observation sheet (see below)

**TRAINEES**
Any

**1** The observer prepares a three-column chart such as the one partly filled in in Figure 22 and completes it during the lesson. If a lesson plan is available, some of the filling in of the 'stage' column can take place before the lesson.

| Stage | Procedure | Alternatives |
|---|---|---|
| 1 Warmer/link with previous lesson | Team game involving Ss in reassembling jumbled sentences exemplifying 2nd conditionals. | |
| 2 Introducing new lexis | Asking Ss if they know words, explaining and demonstrating if they don't. | |
| 3 Listening to tape and Ss doing task (to practise listening for detail) | | |

Fig. 22 The alternatives observation sheet

2 After the lesson, the 'alternatives' column can be filled in by the observer, other trainees, the teacher or any combination of these. It needs to be done in the spirit of gathering options rather than replacing what actually happened by 'better' ideas.

**VARIATIONS**

a The 'stage', 'procedure' and 'alternatives' format can be employed for more detailed observation of a *small part* of a lesson and aided by a video or sound recording or by a lesson transcript so that observer and teacher can focus on exactly what happened.

b The format can be adapted for observation of a particular feature, such as the use of visual aids as in Figure 23.

| Description of use of aid | Reason for using it | Alternatives |
|---|---|---|
| *1. At 6 mins : OHP. Transparency of groundplan of house, left up for 2 mins for Ss to discuss where 7 suspects might be at midnight.* | *To set scene for listening passage to come; to tune Ss in to activity by helping them to visualise the scene.* | |
| *2. At 9 mins: Cassette recorder. T used it to play an account of events leading to a crime, and the crime itself. Played tape twice with different pre-set task for each play through. 5 mins between each play.* | *To give Ss necessary info. for next activity? To give Ss practice in listening for detail?? To provide exposure, as a means of further practice, to language focused on, on previous day.* | |

Fig. 23 Detailed observation of use of aids

**RATIONALE/COMMENT**

This type of record making can encourage non-judgmental observation and discussion of useful future options.112

ACKNOWLEDGEMENT/READING

I learnt this from Peter Maingay. See Freeman (1982), Gebhard (1984) and Maingay (1987).

# UNOBSERVED TEACHING
## Procedure

If you are working with trainees who have been observed a lot recently, why not discuss with them the idea of their working *unobserved* for a lesson or part of a day? If they like the idea, it can be done with:

**a** no task other than to teach the class,
**b** a task negotiated with students, teacher/and or you the trainer,
**c** a task given by you,
**d** all feedback options available, for example:
   - no feedback,
   - feedback between the students and the trainee teacher without the trainer present,
   - the trainee tells another trainee or the trainer how the lesson went and can choose whether or not they wish to have advice, comments and questions. This can take place over coffee after the lesson or while going for a walk and talking together side by side rather than across a table.

### RATIONALE/COMMENT
It is valuable for trainees to experience a normal, natural rapport with a class, that is, without observers present. This 'solo flight' can give confidence.

**5.26**

**MATERIALS**
None

**TRAINEES**
Any

---

# FISHBOWL
## Procedure

### PLANNING THE TEACHING/OBSERVATION
**1** Take one trainee aside. This trainee should speak a language that the other trainees don't, at least well enough to be able to teach the others something useful.
**2** The trainee plans something to teach the others, for example, a set of ten words, a little conversation or a few phrases.
**3** While the trainee is planning, the others in the group organise themselves into two concentric circles. People who would like to learn the foreign language go in the inner circle. People who would just like to watch sit in the outer circle.

### TEACHING/OBSERVATION
**4** The trainee teaches a lesson to the inner circle. People in the outer circle just watch and listen.
**5** Afterwards, there is discussion of how the trainee who taught felt, how the inner circle students felt and how the outer circle people felt.

**5.27**

**MATERIALS**
None

**TRAINEES**
Any, but one of them must know (a bit of) a language unknown to the others

**VARIATIONS**

**a** The trainee who is the teacher gets help from the trainer to teach what they would like to teach in a *new* way, that is, for example, by using the Silent Way or Total Physical Response. Instructions on the method should be minimal so that the teacher can combine the new instructions with their own personality and style.

**b** The people in the outer circle decide to observe for something particular and use a checklist.

**c** Ask the people who have been in the outer circle how much of the target language they remember from 'just' listening and not being taught directly.

**d** The inner and outer circle swap every fifteen minutes, thus each group has a rest from having to interact with the teacher.

**e** The people in the outer circle act as helpers to their opposite numbers in the inner circle. Each helper acts as a prompter for anything their partner in the inner circle has forgotten.

**RATIONALE/COMMENT**

The process here rests on a particular physical arrangement of the group together with peer demonstrations. It is useful because:

**a** People can choose to be more or less active learners.

**b** They see how much is retained by those who have not been taught directly and have not spoken.

**c** People are reminded what it's like to be a language learner, perhaps one who is either concentrated on or ignored by the teacher.

**d** In variation (a), the trainee who teaches has the chance to learn something new.

**e** In variation (b) the teacher has peer feedback on their teaching.

**f** Everyone gets feedback on what it was like to teach, learn and watch.

**g** You can be in either of the circles and so can really be a part of the group for a while.

READING
Rinvolucri (1989).

# Section 4: After the lesson

When I started observing teachers and then meeting them after the lesson to talk about their work, I used to have a fairly set format for the feedback. First, I'd ask them what they thought of their lesson. Then, I'd say what I thought – I'd start with some positive things, raise some more problematic areas and finally finish on an upbeat note. Regardless of the type of lesson I'd seen, that was the way I'd run the feedback session. One day, a teacher in feedback said to me, 'I don't really want to say what I think. And I don't really want a positivity sandwich either. I want to know why it all went dead quiet in the middle of the discussion phase.'

I realised then how fixed and transparent my feedback routine had been. I had only one feedback option in my repertoire. And one wasn't enough for the fifteen very different trainee teachers I was working with.

A couple of years later, after doing lots of homework on this issue, I realised that feedback sessions don't have to be a ritual, or strenuous or harrowing. Here, then, are the ideas I've collected to try to make feedback positive, useful, humane, and . . . varied.

# THE OPTIONS FRAMEWORK

## Procedure

**5.28**

**MATERIALS**
'Options' diagram
(see page 14)

**TRAINEES**
Any

1 Discuss the idea that there are many teaching behaviours possible at any stage of a lesson and that there is no one right way of teaching, but rather many possible options that are all right in some way and certainly right at some time. Link this idea to the 'options' diagram (see page 14 for a fuller explanation of the idea, and also Figure 2 for the diagram).

2 Elicit the sort of language that might be used in a feedback session to go with this idea of teaching as free choice among different tactics. Examples of such language are:
   I decided to do . . ., You did . . ., I had to choose . . ., It was one option . . ., I chose to . . ., The (dis)advantage of it was . . ., What do you feel was the disadvantage of taking that option? Another time I could . . ., Another option available then was . . ., And if I did, the good thing would be . . ., The advantage there might be . . ., But a disadvantage would be . . ., Another time you could choose another option . . ., I'll have to weigh it up . . .

3 Contrast this language with the language often heard in feedback sessions, for example:
   You/I should have . . ., You/I shouldn't have . . ., Why didn't you . . .?, You/I could have . . ., Where you/I went wrong was . . ., I wouldn't have/would have . . ., It was terrible . . ., Everything was OK until you . . ., It wasn't terrible but you . . .

   Points that could be made here are that the language is backward-looking and generally concerned with mistakes, that it implies there is one right way and many ways of going wrong in a lesson.

4 Suggest that during feedback sessions people monitor their own and other people's language to see whether past-looking judgmental phrases are used or whether the more forward-looking, options-based language is used. Include yourself in this experiment.

5 After some feedback sessions ask people how they feel about the two different sorts of language. Which do they prefer or find more helpful? Why?

### RATIONALE/COMMENT

When people feel that there is a right way to do something and lots of wrong ways, they become wary and scared of making mistakes. We know this in language learning. We see students who are over-concerned with accuracy, who stop and start an utterance many times, trying to get everything perfect at once, and often failing to communicate at all. In teacher training this can happen too. Trainees can become over-concerned with getting a set sequence of procedures technically correct regardless of what is actually happening in the classroom.

Thinking of teaching as a series of 'choice-full' options, all of which are right in some way and all of which have their advantages and disadvantages has strong implications for the way feedback is run and for the language used in feedback sessions. It is important that we do not close down or discard teaching options by attacking particular options, but rather discuss them and weigh them up as tactics for future use in different situations.

READING
Woodward (1988c).

## 5.29

**MATERIALS**
None

**TRAINEES**
Ones who have watched each other teach

# WHAT CAN I LEARN FROM YOU?

## Procedure

1 Ask trainees to sit in a circle with you.
2 One trainee goes first. Everyone else, including you, takes it in turns to say one thing they think they can learn from the trainee who goes first. Comments may range from, 'You're always well-organised' to 'I love your drawing' to 'I could learn a lot about looking calm from you' or 'You've got a terrific sense of humour.'
3 While people are talking, the trainee says nothing, not even, 'Oh, thank you!' or 'But I only . . .'
4 Go round the group until every trainee has been addressed (with you included).

### RATIONALE/COMMENT

a In many cultures criticism and self-criticism are highly developed skills which, though useful, can sometimes become a slightly negative habit which tires and demoralises people. This activity encourages public praise. It creates a very good atmosphere and capitalises on the fact that trainees have different strengths and thus can learn from each other.
b It encourages you to learn from trainees too.
c It involves the whole group and is a good morale booster when people are tired, a bit down or about to go off for a weekend or do an exam.

READING
Woodward (1988d).

# ALL AROUND THE CIRCLE TWICE
## Procedure

1 Ask trainees to sit in a circle.
2 Choose one of the trainees who has just taught. Ask them just to listen.
3 People who observed the lesson take it in turns around the circle to state, 'One thing I really liked about your lesson was . . .'
4 After everyone has said something, go round the circle again starting, 'One thing I wondered about was . . .'
5 It's important to remind the observed teacher not to say anything. This prevents them feeling they have to self-deprecate or defend themselves. They can take notes if they like.
6 An optional last step is to allow the observed teacher to comment on anything said.

**VARIATIONS**
a Trainees choose to have the 'I wondered . . .' comments first.
b Individuals can 'pass' if they can't think of anything to say.

**RATIONALE/COMMENT**
a The whole group is involved in observation *and* feedback.
b The observed teacher can just sit, listen, think and take notes.
c It provides a balance of positive and other comments.
d It allows you to hear what others think and usually radically cuts what you have to give as comment on the teaching.

READING
Woodward (1988d).

**5.30**

MATERIALS
None

TRAINEES
Ones who have seen each other teach

# DECOMPRESSION IN PAIRS
## Procedure

1 A trainee who has just taught pairs up with a person who has watched the lesson. They sit somewhere comfortable, out of the classroom if necessary.
2 The observed teacher talks about the lesson – what they felt about it, what worked, what didn't work. They can organise their talk in any way they like. The observer tries to listen as well as possible, using supportive remarks and trying to be genuinely accepting of what is said. The observer is not allowed to make any evaluative comment at all. They only ask questions of fact.
3 (Optional) When the observed teacher has finished talking, the observer recaps what she has heard without any additional comment and with as much of the observed teacher's language as possible.

**5.31**

MATERIALS
None

TRAINEES
Ones who have taught paired with ones who have observed them

**VARIATION**

The person who has taught talks to someone who has not observed their lesson.

**RATIONALE/COMMENT**

**a** This combination of talking and non-judgmental listening allows for a release of nervous energy by the teacher who has just taught and lifts the burden of comment from the listener.

**b** When Step 3 is taken, the observer gets practice in listening to someone's language and repeating it accurately, while the observed teacher hears herself via the observer's echo.

---

## 5.32

**MATERIALS**
None

**TRAINEES**
Any

# THIRTY THINGS I DID

## Procedure

**1** After a teacher has taught, ask her to sit somewhere quietly and write down thirty things that she did in the lesson. The thirty things can be of any type and need not be in chronological order.

**2** Next, the observed teacher writes or comments orally on what would have happened if each of these thirty things had *not* been done.

**RATIONALE/COMMENT**

**a** You can see by looking at the list which things stand out for the trainee.

**b** The number thirty stretches the trainee past obvious comments and into finer details.

**c** By asking the same question of *all* thirty items (i.e. 'What would have happened if you hadn't done this?'), the activity becomes non-judgmental.

**d** It is useful for expanding consciousness of options versus traditions and 'rules'.

ACKNOWLEDGEMENT
I learnt this from Seth Lindstromberg.

---

## 5.33

**MATERIALS**
None

**TRAINEES**
This works best with trainees who have observed each other teach

# WHO COULD HAVE USED IT?

## Procedure

**1** After a group of trainees have taught and, preferably, observed each other, they settle into a circle.

**2** Demonstrate a new technique, for example, a way of eliciting student-to-student correction or a way of calling out questions to make students work while the teacher is writing on the board.

**3** Ask, 'Who could have used this technique in their lesson if you had known about it?' and 'When could you have used it?'.

**4** Trainees mentally go through their lessons trying to fit in the new technique in retrospect. If one trainee finds she can, then she acts out the changed sequence for the group. That is, she redoes part of the lesson using the new technique.

**5** Discussion follows on the new technique, its uses past and future and useful ways of fitting it in to a lesson.

**RATIONALE/COMMENT**

**a** Teachers have to remember their lessons in detail.

**b** An idea is transmitted but not in an input session. Thus, this is a way of integrating input and feedback in one session.

**c** Trainees appear to find much normal input remote because it is typically timetabled to come *before* any opportunity to apply it. This training process allows trainees to apply the new idea to their own work straight away and may, therefore, lead them to incorporate the idea faster than usual into their 'permanent' repertoire.

ACKNOWLEDGEMENT
I learnt this from Seth Lindstromberg.

# THE TRAINER RECEIVES FEEDBACK
## Procedure

**5.34**

**MATERIALS**
Any observation checklists or rating schedules usually used on the trainees

**1** Before a normal input session or workshop organised and taught by you, give out any observation tasks, checklists or rating schedules that you usually use while watching your trainee(s) teach.

**2** Ask one, or some, trainees to use these while observing your input session.

**3** When the session is over, allow some time for the observing trainee(s) to complete their notes.

**4** The trainee(s) give(s) feedback to you on your teaching.

**TRAINEES**
Any who have all had input and supervision from the same trainer

**VARIATION**

Different trainees can be observers in input sessions at different times in the same session or in different input sessions. This way everyone has a chance to observe you and give you feedback on different aspects of your teaching/training.

**RATIONALE/COMMENT**

In this simple reversals idea:

**a** You learn how it feels to receive feedback.

**b** Trainees learn how it feels to give feedback.

**c** Whatever spirit is prevalent in feedback normally shows up in this feedback too, but in this case might be more noticeable to you. After using this training process, you might want to make some adjustments to the normal feedback sessions.

## 5.35

**MATERIALS**
A video or sound
recording of a
lesson

**TRAINEES**
Any

# ANALYSIS OF TAPES

## Procedure

1 A video or sound recording of part or all of a trainee's lesson is made.
2 After the lesson the trainee listens to/watches the tape and analyses it
for any of the features below. (It is as well to analyse a tape or part of
a tape for one feature at a time. Once trainees get used to analysing
tapes, they can work on several features at once.)
   a phrases used to praise, greet the class, start or stop groupwork, etc.
     – is there a good repertoire or are there some strong verbal tics?
   b times when students corrected themselves before being corrected
     by the teacher,
   c percentage of student and teacher talking time,
   d times when there seemed to be communicational harmony be-
     tween two students or a student and the teacher,
   e the number of times the teacher chooses particular students to
     answer questions or the number of Yes/No versus open questions,
   f the number of unprompted student contributions,
   g times when the teacher seemed to really notice a student contribu-
     tion,
   h what *exactly* is said by students in the mother tongue (this can
     form the basis of the next lesson's content),
   i times when a student's eyes or posture tell a different story from
     their words,
   j the effectiveness of teacher responses in further discussion,
   k the clarity, pitch, interest and volume of the teacher's voice,
   l times when the teacher sounds like somebody's parent,
   m what correction techniques are used,
   n times when the teacher looks distinctly uncomfortable,
   o number of silences,
   p proportion of the language that is meaningful versus meaningless.
   Alternatively, the trainee can listen to the tape once, without prior
   aims, simply noting anything of interest that comes up.
3 Trainees highlight any snippet of a tape by playing it at the feedback
session or by producing a short transcription of some exchanges that
are particularly interesting to them.
4 Trainees decide what to change in their teaching, for example, they
may wish to aim for a broader range of phrases for marking the
boundaries between phases of their lessons. They try to introduce
this change into their teaching and then retape to see what progress
they have made.

### RATIONALE/COMMENT

a Some teachers may prefer sound to video taping because language
students are used to tape recorders in the classroom and so sound
recording is not disruptive to a class. Sound taping is also cheap and
uncomplicated. If short parts of a lesson are taped, it is not too time
consuming.

**b** Hearing and seeing is believing. Sometimes trainees will grasp a point about their own teaching *only* when they hear or see themselves at work. Alternatively, trainees may have a prejudice about their own teaching that is *not* borne out by the real tape data.

**c** Once trainees become practised and skilled at analysing their own teaching tapes, they can carry on doing this on their own.

READING
Woodward (1989b).

# ADDITIONAL WAYS OF STRUCTURING FEEDBACK SESSIONS

## Procedure

**5.36**

**TRAINEES**
Any

To help prevent feedback sessions from becoming routinised or too predictable in their structure, here are some ideas for altering their format:

**a** The observer states what she thinks of the lesson observed. The person who taught just listens.

**b** The observer asks the observed teacher what she thought of her lesson. Afterwards, the observer adds her comments.

**c** Trainees, in pairs, give each other feedback based on different types of observation task (see Section 3 *During observations*). People keep switching pairs until everyone has been in one-to-one feedback with everyone else.

**d** Those who have observed and taught go for a short walk together or alone to ponder the lesson in question, relax a bit and prioritise comments and questions.

**e** Observers leave the room in order to allow the language students to give the trainee(s) feedback on their lesson(s)

**f** Lessons are discussed in answer to one question, 'What did the language students learn?'

**g** After input on a particular micro-skill (e,g, asking gist questions, dialogue building, pattern practice), a trainee tries out the new technique in the observed lesson. Feedback is then only a discussion of the *technique* and what teacher and student pleasures or difficulties were associated with it.

**h** Hand out to trainees your written notes of whatever kind. Trainees then take time to read these notes and talk to each other about the observed lesson using the notes as a basis and saying what they agree or disagree with.

**i** Ask trainees to think for a moment and to prepare one thing to say, and only one, that they feel would help the teacher who has just taught. All trainees say their one thing to the teacher. The observed teacher just listens and makes notes if they wish.

**j** Trainees give you full feedback on your input sessions using any style of feedback and based on any observation task they wish.

**k** The person who has taught prepares three questions they would like to ask the observer(s). Each observer prepares one question they would like to ask the teacher. After this preparation time, the observed teacher asks her questions first and observers answer. If the observer's question has not come up yet, then she asks it and the observed teacher answers.

**l** Each trainee is responsible for doing something different. Or, if only one trainee is involved, she is responsible for a different thing in each observation, for example, recalling the steps of the lesson, reporting on instruction, reporting on error correction and so on (see Section 3 *During observations* for ideas here).

**m** Give trainees your feedback sheets fully filled in except for the 'Conclusions' or 'General comments' section. It is the trainees' job to fill in this concluding section.

## 5.37

**TRAINEES**
Any

# WAYS OF ENDING FEEDBACK

## Procedure

After feedback has been given, in any of the ways described in this section so far, it can be important to round things off by:

**a** asking each observed teacher to say which of all the comments made on her lesson she remembers most,

**b** asking each observed teacher to remember one good thing about her teaching, and one thing to work on,

**c** asking teachers to restate to the group or write down for themselves the main points mentioned in the feedback,

**d** asking teachers to tell you or to write down what they will be working on next time,

**e** brainstorming specific things that each teacher can do to work on the area that's troubling her,

**f** asking each trainee to remember one good thing about her lesson, to keep this in her mind for a full minute and to recall it just before she goes to sleep at night,

**g** encouraging trainees, if feedback has been difficult or lessons haven't gone well, to think of it as 'just *one* bad lesson' which the students will already have forgotten,

**h** finishing off with a friendly, supportive, encouraging or upbeat remark,

**i** talking about completely different things to finish off, preferably an area that the trainees find pleasant and rewarding such as a hobby or an event they are looking forward to.

**RATIONALE/COMMENT**

**a** The selective recall, statement and problem solving here remind trainees of the main points of a feedback and give ways of tackling the areas they want to, or have to, work on.

**b** Trainees' spirits are lifted and they are encouraged to think positively when they leave the group. This may help prevent people from leaving the feedback feeling so tense that they are unable to sleep at night and or generally lift their mood.

**c** Trainees are encouraged to remember that teaching and feedback are just one small part of their lives.

**d** There may be trainees who do not wish to have the sort of 'closure' that I advocate here. Some may want to draw their own boundaries in their own ways, for example, by leaving early or by talking about a problem or joy they themselves have in another area of life, or by ignoring the trainer and focusing on fellow trainees. It goes without saying that the trainees' desire for no closure or different closure is to be respected.

# *Postscript to Chapter 5: A review of major options*

I started off this chapter by suggesting that we all have our own normal ways of handling lesson planning, observation and feedback. As you read through this chapter you may have come across ideas that are very different from your normal practice. It is perhaps precisely these ideas that will have the most important implications about what is and what is not 'normal' for you. I'd like to look next at some of the major implications of the ideas in this chapter.

## Implications for the role of the observer

We normally think of the trainer as the observer, but, in fact, the trainer can be the observed and the trainees the observers. Observing need not be done in order to assess someone. Instead, observers can watch for what teachers or students have asked them to watch for. Alternatively, they can simply *describe* classroom events, language and types of interaction in a non-evaluative, factual fashion.

Observers' work can be of use to the *language student* as a record of their linguistic/communicative progress, to the *teacher* as a mirror and of use to *you*, the trainer, too since it helps if there are more pairs of eyes and ears in a lesson than yours alone. Surprisingly (perhaps), using varied observation tasks tends to be of most use to the observer, since using different tasks refines the observer's view of what they see, helps them to understand that it is not only the teacher's behaviour that is worth watching, and gets them into the useful habit of observing and describing learning and teaching events. Trainee observers can continue this increase in depth of description when working on their own or with colleagues later.

An observer can be quietly watching and drawing or noting, can join in the lesson to help out with pairwork or monitoring, or can intervene to help the teacher if the teacher wants.

## The focus of the observation

Observers (whether peers, language students or the trainer) can look at a language student or students or they can look at activities, materials, classroom positions or organisation. That is, they need not focus totally on the person teaching. They can focus on teacher language, student language, student strategies or teacher strategies. They can look for concentration, for loss of concentration or for stress. Interactions of different types can be noted and an eye for alternative strategies kept open.

## Keeping records

Records need not be kept on pro-forma, in-house observation sheets alone. Information, or 'classroom data', can be recorded on tape or on paper, in the form of graphs, diagrams, notes, questions, letters, checklists, grids or little boxes.

## Feedback

Feedback does not have to be one-to-one, trainer to trainee, or judgmental. It can be complimentary, supportive, varied in content, organisation and aim, and positive. It can include input, planning and analysis. It *can* close all options down and work towards 'the one right way of teaching' or it can open out alternatives for both the observer and the observed.

# CHAPTER 6

# *Finding out*

A training course or workshop is usually a time when lots of different people come to do things together. It is, therefore, a perfect place for people to learn about themselves, about each other, and about the work they intend to do. On many courses, time is allowed for personal contact to be made, for networks to form, for questions to be asked and curiosity satisfied. On some courses, this may happen in a timetabled warm-up phase or, informally, in tea breaks and after course meetings. But it is also possible to use the natural curiosity and natural networking, and integrate it systematically throughout the course. This chapter details some ways that course participants can be actively encouraged to find out about other people, about themselves and about the job of language teaching as an integral part of the course. It thus gives this work an importance by allowing it some 'prime time'.

# Section 1: Finding out about yourself and others

## 6.1

**MATERIALS**
None

**TRAINEES**
See comment **d**

## ANSWERING FOR SOMEONE ELSE

### Procedure

1 Split the class into two semi-circles facing each other. Put all the people who know each other into same semi-circle A.

2 Choose one person in semi-circle A to be the 'sitter'. This person sits inside semi-circle A with the people who know her. The sitter faces the people in the other semi-circle. (See Figure 24.)

*Semi-circle A*                    *Semi-circle B*

Fig. 24 Seating arrangement

3 The participants in semi-circle B ask the sitter questions. The questions can be on any subject, for example:
  • semi-personal: 'Are you married?', 'Do you have any pets?', 'Do you like gardening?'
  • about teaching situations: 'Do you teach adults or children?', 'Do you have your own room or do you move from classroom to classroom?'
  • about teaching beliefs: 'What is the best way to deal with discipline problems?'
  The sitter does not answer. Rather, any participant in semi-circle A who feels they know how the sitter might answer, answers for her. If the answer is accurate, the sitter nods. If the answer is totally wrong, she shakes her head. If the answer is not quite accurate, the sitter tips her head or gives a 'doubtful' sign with her hand. If the sitter indicates an answer was wrong or doubtful, another trainee in semi-circle A can give another answer. If this one is closer to the truth, the sitter nods. If no one seems to know how the sitter might answer, semi-circle A asks for the next question.

4 After the trainees in semi-circle B have asked all the questions they want, the sitter goes back into semi-circle A and comments, if she wants to, on what was accurate or inaccurate about the answers. She can also answer for herself any questions that her semi-circle was completely unable to answer on her behalf.

5 The activity continues with a new person from semi-circle A taking the role of sitter. And it can go on for as long as appropriate on one day or can be done over several days with different sitters until, possibly, everyone in the group has been the sitter.

### VARIATIONS

The basic idea here is that people can answer for other people. Participants can do this for each other, as above, or:

a for the trainer,

b for students in their classes,

c for their bosses,

d for examiners, or for others.

### RATIONALE/COMMENT

a People find out how much they know about others.

b Sitters find out how much people know about them.

c The quality of listening tends to be higher in this activity than when people answer questions for themselves.

d This process idea is especially useful for times when some people in a group know each other very well, but know other people only slightly, if at all. So it's good when remnants of two different classes come together, or when a trainer comes to a group composed of some participants who know her well and others who do not know her at all.

ACKNOWLEDGEMENT

I learnt this activity from Rod Bolitho.


# BASIC QUESTIONS

## Procedure

**6.2**

**MATERIALS**
None

**TRAINEES**
Trainees who have just started a training course and who do not know each other well

1 Ask trainees to write down the following questions:
- What teaching or other work experience do you have?
- Why have you come on this course?
- What can you offer to the course – what strengths do you have?
- What are you hoping/going to do after the course?
- Tell me something you think the group or the trainer(s) should know about you.

2 Ask trainees to take a moment to think and write down any other questions they would like to put to other people in the group.

3 Ask trainees one by one to dictate their additional questions to the group. If there are two similar questions from different trainees, negotiate a single version. In either case people only write down in dictation the extra questions that they feel are interesting.

   Each trainee should now have a list of questions, some given by you and some by others in the group.

4 Trainees pair up and ask each other their questions. Allow plenty of time for these interviews (perhaps fifteen minutes).

**5** The interviewing phase stops after one pairing or people can re-pair again and find out about more than one other person in the group.

### VARIATIONS

**a** Instead of you providing the first five questions, all the questions can come from the trainees.

**b** The idea of trainee-generated questions can be used mid-term for evaluation and course assessment purposes.

### RATIONALE/COMMENT

Activities such as 'Search for/Find someone who . . .' (see Moskowitz 1978) can tend to confine new groups to rather superficial and fleeting question-and-answer encounters. *Basic questions* allows people to get down to essentials immediately.

### ACKNOWLEDGEMENT

This is a blend of ideas I learnt from trainees represented at the Trainee Voices Day of the IATEFL Teacher Training Special Interest Group (London, November 1990).

---

## 6.3

**MATERIALS**
A board, flipchart or OHP are best, but this can be done with just a notebook

**TRAINEES**
Any

# GROUP PROFILE GAME

## Procedure

**1** Everyone sits in a circle. A 'scribe' is nominated.

**2** Any participant can put a question to the whole group such as, 'I wonder how many vegetarians there are in the group' or 'I'd like to know if anybody comes by car from X.'

**3** After each question, people respond. For example, in answer to the first question above, a few people might put up their hands and say, 'I am!' In answer to the second, someone might put up their hand and say, 'Well, I don't come from X but I drive through it on my way here.'

**4** The scribe records facts about the group on the board. For example, 'There are four vegetarians in the group.' 'Nobody in the group comes from X but one person drives through it on their way to Y.'

**5** Individuals put as many questions to the whole group as they like. Questions can also be about work experiences (e.g. 'How many people here work in classes of over fifty pupils?') or resources ('Who has some pictures I could use for teaching the comparative?') or attitudes ('Does everybody here think the Silent Way is only for beginners?').

**6** At the end of the question period, a group profile has been built up in the form of the recorded statements. These can be read out loud or written on a wall poster. Discussion can follow.

## VARIATIONS

**a** Instead of one scribe recording the information about the group, each individual in the group can record the information for herself.

**b** This process of posing one's own questions to the group can be repeated several times during the life of a group. The types of question change as the group changes.

**c** Different groups, who are going to meet later, can type up and exchange the profiles they have made. This usually arouses interest in advance. The groups will want to find out who the mysterious 'one person in our group . . .' is, or why there are so many people in the group who hate using tape recorders, and so on.

**d** A group can keep their profile for comparison with later profiles to learn how they have changed.

**e** The language area implied (e.g. *all of us, some of us, none of us, nearly everybody*, etc.) is a rich and useful one for non-native speaker trainees to work on.

## RATIONALE/COMMENT

**a** Individuals can find out whether they are in a majority or a minority on any issue.

**b** People can use the activity to gets lifts to class, find squash partners, get rid of extra theatre tickets, borrow books, or catch up on good notes from a lecture they missed – in other words, to get what they want from the group. This obviously includes the trainer too, who can ask questions such as, 'How many people found the lecture on X too difficult?'

**c** The activity encourages a group spirit.


# WHY ARE WE HERE?

## Procedure

1 The trainees write down, on three separate slips of paper, three different reasons why they have come to the workshop, session or course.

2 They stand up and mill around talking to people. The aim is to get rid of all three of their own slips of paper (not necessarily at the same time) by bartering them for other people's slips of paper. Participants can only exchange one of their own slips for someone else's if they find someone who has a reason that is as good for them as their own. Thus, someone who wrote, 'I'm here to improve my English' could exchange with someone who wrote, 'My husband was coming this way by car anyway so I thought I might as well come', if it happened to be true that *they*'d had a lift with their husband.

3 Once most people have got rid of their own slips and gained three new ones, they can read out or quote reasons they liked or found unusual.

**6.4**

**MATERIALS**
None

**TRAINEES**
Those with different reasons for attending

### VARIATIONS

You can use this bartering process with other questions, for example: 'What would you be doing if you weren't here?', 'What do you know about . . .?, 'What will you be doing this time tomorrow/next week?', 'What can you give to the group?', 'What do you want from this course/session?', 'What makes a good teacher?', 'What exercises are good for encouraging fluency?' etc.

### RATIONALE/COMMENT

**a** The topic chosen in the main activity gets rid of nerves at the start of a session by bringing out into the open all the ambivalences people usually have about giving up time to attend courses.

**b** It is a good way for people to find out that other people are as cranky, optimistic, pessimistic, or ambivalent as themselves.

**c** The final sharing of comments can dispel any misconceptions you may have had as to why people have come.

**d** The extraordinary thing about this activity is (1) how many reasons are usually produced, and (2) how often it is possible to trade reasons with someone.

**e** If the course/workshop is compulsory for all trainees, then of course the exercise won't work!

ACKNOWLEDGEMENT

I learnt this technique from Richard Baudains, who introduced it as a workshop opener for negotiating expectations.

---

**6.5**

**MATERIALS**
None

**TRAINEES**
Any, especially
non-native

# INSISTENCE QUESTIONS
## Procedure

**1** To demonstrate the activity, ask participants to ask you the same questions again and again, allowing time for you to reply each time. You set the question, for example, 'Why did you become a teacher?' Answer truthfully, but in a different way each time, for example:

P1  Why did you become a teacher?
T    Because I was near a place where I could get training.
P2  Why did you become a teacher?
T    Because I wanted to.
P3  Why did you become a teacher?
T    Because I'd come to the end of the line in my previous job.
P4  Why did you become a teacher?
T    Because I thought I'd be a better one than some of my own teachers.

**2** Once you've run out of answers (after at least ten) encourage discussion on any point of the activity that participants do not understand. They can also follow up any of the answers that intrigued them, for example, 'What was your previous job? You said you'd come to the end of the line with it.'

**3** Once participants have got the idea, they can work in pairs or small groups, taking it in turns to be the questioner. Again, answers need to be true, many and different. When the answerer cannot think of any more answers, they can say, 'I give up!' It is important that everyone gets the chance to be an answerer.

### VARIATIONS

The question used can vary, for example: 'When do you like teaching?', 'When do you dislike teaching?', 'What do you do with tapes in the classroom?', 'What's the difference between the way you normally teach and the method we've seen today?', 'What's the difference between Halliday and Chomsky?', 'What would you like to change in your teaching from now on?' (See also 2.17 *Starter question circle*.)

### RATIONALE/COMMENT

This activity capitalises on the fact that there are usually hundreds of possible and partial answers inside us for each question we are asked. We usually sigh inwardly and choose one answer to suit the audience, knowing that we have not answered fully. But in this exercise, we have the chance to bring out *all* the answers. This activity is especially good for stretching the repertoire of non-native speaking trainees past the usual well-practised but often rather superficial answers to everyday questions.

ACKNOWLEDGEMENT
This idea comes from Frank and Rinvolucri (1983 p. 54).

## TWO USUAL QUESTIONS, TWO UNUSUAL QUESTIONS 6.6

## Procedure

**MATERIALS**
None

**TRAINEES**
Any who do not know each other very well

**1** Ask participants to pair up with someone they do not know at all or who they know very little.

**2** Arrange a stopping signal that participants will be able to see or hear later above the noise, for example, a shimmer of a tambourine, or the lights switching on and off.

**3** People ask each other two usual questions (e.g. 'What's your name?' and 'Where do you work?') and two unusual questions (e.g. 'Where did you buy that shirt?', 'How do you squeeze your toothpaste tube?', 'Where would you be if you hadn't come here today?'). Ask them to try to remember each other's answers.

**4** When people have had enough time to ask each other the four questions, stop them with the pre-arranged signal.

**5** Next, ask the pair to remain together but to go to meet another pair, so making a foursome. If there are any pairs left over, they need to join with a four to make a group of six.

**6** In the foursome, people do not ask questions or talk about themselves, but introduce their partner to the other people in their group.

So one of a pair will say, 'Can I introduce you to Mildred? Mildred comes from Oslo and she told me that she'd be gardening now if she hadn't . . .' Those being introduced can interrupt to contradict any untruths about themselves made because the partner had misheard or misremembered, or misunderstood.

7 (Optional) A foursome goes to meet another foursome, so making eight. Again, people introduce others rather than themselves. They can introduce a different person this time. This 'pyramid technique' of 1+1=2, 2+2=4, 4+4=8, etc. can, of course, keep going until a plenary is reached, but I usually stop it at four, for time reasons.

### VARIATIONS

a Instead of asking each other 'getting-to-know-you' questions, the original pairs talk about their understanding of a text or lecture, about teaching teminology or about other course content.

b Instead of 'usual' and 'unusual', the categories could be 'easy' and 'difficult', or questions about 'productive' and 'receptive' skills, etc.

### RATIONALE/COMMENT

a At the start of a course, when people are shy, the main activity allows them to make contact with one other person first and then to take this new friend into a slightly wider group.

b It encourages people to listen to each other so they can recap later.

c People tend to listen especially carefully when they are being talked about.

## 6.7

**MATERIALS**
None

**TRAINEES**
Any, although I feel it works better with in-service trainees

**TRAINER**
Experienced, flexible, sensitive and preferably with some counselling skills

# A PSYCHODRAMA MODEL

It can be quite difficult to find interesting ways of discovering exactly what trainees' hopes, aims and goals really are. The following idea is an unusual one in that it asks trainees to move into the role of trainer and to talk about themselves as trainees. This role switch may be quite startling for the trainee who hears herself diagnosing her own strengths and weaknesses out loud. It can be very revealing for a trainer and can prevent the trainer from making assumptions and projections about what trainees need. By involving the trainees in their own diagnosis and thus giving both trainee and trainer valuable information, it is hoped that the trainers will make their work more relevant to trainees. It might help trainees to work at a deeper level, too, taking the course seriously in terms of personal development rather than just attending and keeping the course 'at arm's length'.

## Procedure

1 Everyone sits in a circle.
2 You go up to a trainee, for example, Mrs Fran Singer, shake her by the hand and invite her to stand up.

**3** You say, 'So, Mrs Singer, you are Fran's teacher trainer. And this is Fran', and here you gesture towards the chair just vacated by the participant.

**4** You continue, 'Tell me, as a colleague, trainer to trainer, why did Fran come on this course?' The dialogue might develop like this:

F   Er . . . Fran felt her teaching had gone really stale.

T   Was she right? Had it?

F   In some ways . . . yes.

T   Well, trainer, if you agree that it had, it suggests that something was not going very well in classes. What was wrong with Fran's teaching?

**5** The participant gives a fuller self-diagnosis, not omitting to suggest remedies for any difficulties.

**6** Go around the circle treating each participant as her main trainer.

### VARIATIONS

**a** The questions can relate to any aspect of teaching or learning, for example, 'What does Fran think about translation?', 'What does Fran really think about doing pairwork in her large class of sixty pupils?'

**b** Instead of putting a trainee in role as her own trainer, address her as one of her students.

### RATIONALE/COMMENT

**a** In this role-play process of talking out loud about yourself, the trainer and other participants find out a great deal. It can be easier too for the trainees to express some of their real thoughts when they are role playing someone other than themselves.

**b** The trainee is transformed from a person who is 'done to' into a powerful, self-responsible person discussing her own strengths and weaknesses and suggesting her own diagnoses and solutions.

Here are excerpts from comments two in-service trainees made about themselves in relation to the Royal Society of Arts Diploma in TEFL course they were in:

*Trainee 1*

'Well, she needs to work harder. She's not dedicated enough. Generally, she gets most of her assignments in on time although the last one hasn't . . . er . . . turned up yet! I've noticed a difference in her since the start of the course. She started off very enthusiastic. But she's under a lot of pressure at school. She has to do a lot of social activities. She's put upon. You see, there are only five members of staff in her school. The others are married. She's one of the youngest and only lives a few doors away from the school, so she's under pressure to do most of the social stuff.'

*Trainee 2*

'Well, a bit like the last trainee said, my person started off the course full of enthusiasm. He did a lot of work even *before* the course, reading and writing notes and questions. He thought the course would be a doddle. He thought too much of his own ability. Yes, he had a high opinion of himself before he started.

Now he's not sure. His confidence has taken a bit of a knock. It's probably just a phase. It's winter and he gets very depressed in winter. He'll probably be all right but . . . er . . . he's not so sure about things now.'

ACKNOWLEDGEMENT/READING
I learnt this idea from Mario Rinvolucri (see Rinvolucri 1987) who learnt it from Greta Leutz (see Leutz 1985).

## 6.8

**MATERIALS**
A class set of copies of a handwritten letter from you to your trainees

**TRAINEES**
Any

# LETTERS BETWEEN TRAINER AND TRAINEES

## Procedure

1 Write a general open letter, preferably in handwriting, telling people a little about yourself. Give a copy to everyone, either in or out of class. Invite anyone who likes writing letters to respond.
2 You should get a few letters in reply.
3 Treat them as normal, private correspondence by replying to them without correction and without showing them to others or referring to their contents openly in the group. The corresondence may continue and develop, or it may fizzle out after it has served its purpose, as any correspondence can.

Not everyone will want to write. That's OK. It should not be compulsory.

**VARIATIONS**
a Participants can write letters to each other.
b A trainer can write to another trainer.
c A trainer can write to herself.
d Letters can touch on professional issues such as: encounters with students or colleagues, steps taken in class, books and ideas, or can consist of transcriptions of conversations in class with hints or feedback.
e Letter writing can take place in class or out.

**RATIONALE/COMMENT**
a You have, in a sense, some 'alone time' with the trainee/correspondent. This is rare on a busy training course and often impossible face to face except in tutorials or at coffee breaks.
b You and the participant can find out about each other in a very different way from usual. Different things come out via writing than via speech or in front of the whole group.

ACKNOWLEDGEMENTS
I first experienced this letter-writing process when I responded, as a participant, to an open letter from Mario Rinvolucri, who was at that time my trainer. I then experienced letter writing between peers, in class time, with Mike Gradwell, who was leading a workshop.

# MEMBER OF THE WEEK
## Procedure

1 For a group that meets regularly, set aside some time during each meeting for one person to say something about themselves. You can start off if necessary. The person talking can talk about anything they like.

    Some people will choose to talk about how they got into teaching, some will want to tell people about their new baby, some will tell the entire story of their lives, others will talk about something they have read recently, and so on.

2 While the person is talking, the entire group listens as carefully as possible, without comment.

3 At the end of the talk, people may ask questions.

4 When the talker has finished, the trainer thanks her and the meeting goes on or breaks for coffee, or whatever, as appropriate.

5 At the next meeting, a different person becomes 'member of the week'. The new person can be a volunteer or can be chosen by the group.

### RATIONALE/COMMENT

a This process of gently spotlighting one person is excellent for long-standing staffrooms where people have the feeling that they know everything about each other but in fact rarely take the time to really listen to each other.

b It is also good for groups where people know that they don't know each other very well.

ACKNOWLEDGEMENT/READING
I learnt this technique from Natalie Hess. (See Hess 1989.)

## 6.9
**MATERIALS**
None

**TRAINEES**
Any

# WHAT'S YOUR CLASSROOM LIKE?
## Procedure

1 Give out one large sheet of paper (about A3 size) to each participant and put coloured pens where they can reach them.

2 Ask them to call to mind the classroom they always teach in, one they often teach in or a typical classroom that they work in.

3 Ask participants to draw a plan of this room and mark in walls, doors and windows first.

4 Once they have done this, ask people to mark in the following things little by little as they draw (some things they can draw, some they can indicate by writing on the drawing or by adding footnotes):
- the desks (including vacant ones),
- the position of any equipment (e.g. boards, OHP, tape recorders, or bunsen burners, etc. if the class is held in a science lab),

## 6.10
**MATERIALS**
Large sheets of paper; plenty of coloured pens; cassette recorder; music tapes

**TRAINEES**
Practising teachers from different backgrounds

- the teacher's usual position (with a dotted line for where they usually walk or can get to),
- what can be seen from the window,
- what the heating/cooling system looks like and if it's efficient,
- the lighting system,
- noticeable/memorable colours,
- what's next door,
- a few notes on the type of students,
- any other features participants feel are important.

While the trainees are working on the task, you can play music in the background. Allow plenty of time and give out new paper if people want to start again.

5 Ask participants to mark onto their plans anything else they would like to.

6 Once everybody has finished, ask people to pair up with someone whose drawing is very different from their own. The pairs explain their drawings to each other.

7 People may ask supplementary questions in their pairs, such as 'What do you like/dislike most about your classroom?'

8 Once discussion is over, pin up all the plans where they can be seen. Everybody can now promenade and look at the plans.

### EXTENSION

9 You can keep the plans up on the wall and refer to them during the course. For example, you stand by one plan and ask, 'How would we have to adapt that idea for Geeta's classroom?' or 'I'm not sure we could do that in Renu's room. Can we adapt it?'

10 At the end of the course all participants take home someone else's plan. That way, they can remember the person and remind themselves that others work in very different surroundings.

### VARIATION

The same idea can be used for 'What's your staffroom like?' For some people this will entail drawing a simple bulletin board, for others, a luxurious, carpeted lounge.

### RATIONALE/COMMENT

a This process aims to bring the reality of teachers' working lives visibly into the training room. This can help you to make the course more relevant and useful to the participants.

b The different drawings show up the differences in people's situations. This can help people to understand why different people in the group are asking different questions or balking at certain activities.

c It is also a useful spur to discussing adaptations and variations to ideas that have been introduced.

# THE MARKET PLACE

## Procedure

6.11
**MATERIALS**
Pen and paper

**TRAINEES**
People with
teaching
experience

1 Talk about market places you've been to in different countries. Ask participants to talk about their experiences too – the colours, the noise, the smells. Explain that there will be a market place on the course too!

2 Ask the participants to write down a list of the things that they have as teachers – things that they can do and can show, talk about, and teach to others.

3 After they've written their lists, participants should write a 'shopping list'; that is, a list of things they haven't got but would like to have professionally. Now everyone, including you, has two lists, one of the things they have and one of the things they want.

4 Some people stay still – sitting or standing – and some people move around. (People can choose which group they'd prefer to belong to.)

At this stage, people chat about what they have and what they need. This may lead to some participants changing their lists a little as they realise that they are good at something they had forgotten, or as they remember that they too need something they hear someone else mention.

Allow plenty of time for this phase.

5 Gently come back into a plenary. Try, as a group, to find out what the gluts and dearths are. Ask who found someone who has what they want. Ask who didn't find anyone. Try to establish roughly what numbers are interested in particular subjects.

6 What happens next depends on the way you run your course.

a If the course is intensive or residential, you can next set up a 'market place' notice board. Individuals offer short informal workshops on anything they feel confident about. The workshops can last from ten minutes to an hour or so. Everyone pins up a sheet of paper giving details of their planned workshop. Other people sign up if they'd like to attend. These people then make a time and date to get together. You need to make sure they have a space to meet in and any materials they need.

b Alternatively, a certain part of each course can be set aside for these 'swap shops' to happen.

I have found that they work best if (1) they are outside course time, (2) they are very informal, (3) the trainers do not *automatically* attend, but rather participants and trainers alike offer workshops sometimes and attend sometimes, but only when they are really interested.

With lively groups, the 'market place' system leads to a constant whirl of short, interesting and useful workshops that spark off ideas, friendships and more workshops.

7 If a workshop throws up a large number of questions that the participants feel are really important, the topic can move onto the main programme. Workshop participants can show how far they've got and other sources of information can be brought in to help out.

### RATIONALE/COMMENT

**a** This process of expressing out loud your own professional 'balance sheet' works against the idea that peole come to a course 'empty' and wait to be 'filled'. It accepts that everyone present knows some things and doesn't know others.

**b** Some people need the self-affirmation of teaching before they can learn completely.

**c** What people need and want comes out in this activity and this can help course planning.

**d** The trainee workshops can be very useful to participants and confidence-boosting to the trainee who gives them. They also provide a separate energy and resource to the trainer's input.

## 6.12

**MATERIALS**
Pen and slips of paper

**TRAINEES**
Any

# I WISH I . . .

## Procedure

1 Give each trainee three slips of paper, or ask them each to prepare their own.

2 On each slip of paper they write a sentence about themselves as a teacher or trainer. On the first slip of paper the sentence would start with the words:
*'I wish I was . . .'*
On the second, the trainees write a sentence starting:
*'I wish I had . . .'*
The third sentence begins:
*'I wish I could . . .'*

3 Everybody folds their slips in half, then drops each onto a different one of three separate piles formed on the floor in the middle of the room. There is one pile for all the sentences starting, *'I wish I was . . .'* and so on. Mix and shuffle each pile.

4 Everybody takes one slip at random out of each of the three piles.

5 People take it in turns to read out the three slips they've picked up. Others can make comments on the composite 'personality' expressed by each set of three slips.

### VARIATIONS

There are many other good sentence starters besides *'I wish . . .'*, for example:

**a** *'I can/can't . . .'*, *'I wish I could . . .'* (for identifying needs)

**b** *'I have . . .'*, *'I haven't . . .'*, *'I wish I had . . .'* (also for identifying needs).

**c** *'I understand . . .'*, *'I don't understand . . .'*, *'I think I understand . . .'* this is especially good for use at the beginning or end of an input session.

**RATIONALE/COMMENT**

a If used at the start of a course or session, this individual written completions process can give an interesting profile of the sorts of wants and needs existing in the group.

b The use of sentence starters forces trainees to plunge straight into a topic and reveal more in a shorter time than perhaps they normally would. Nobody is forced to reveal anything they don't wish to reveal, however.

ACKNOWLEDGEMENT

I learnt this from Peter Grundy.


# COMPLETING SENTENCES ABOUT EACH OTHER

## Procedure

**6.13**

**MATERIALS**
Pens and slips of paper

**TRAINEES**
This process works with trainees who don't know each other very well (but who are prepared to guess!) and with those who do know each other well.

1 Using sentence 'middles' such as the ones below, people work in pairs to write sentences about each other, either from personal knowledge or from guesswork. They write each sentence on a separate slip of paper.

   *. . . gets more satisfaction from . . .*
   *. . . is worried about . . .*
   *. . . is very good at . . .*
   *. . . would like to . . .*

2 Partners look at each other's slips in pairs to see if they agree with the wording and content of each sentence.

**VARIATIONS**

a Other sentence parts can be used, for example:

   *. . . hopes that this session won't . . .*
   *. . . thinks that drills are . . .*

b The slips can be kept and looked at later in the workshop or course and discussed. Has there been any change?

c People write on slips of paper a *question* they would like someone to ask them. They then hand the question to a partner. The partner asks them the question.

**RATIONALE/COMMENT**

a This communal written completions process swiftly eases people into deeper issues than names and job status.

b People have the chance to speculate, take risks and check their speculations.

ACKNOWLEDGEMENT

I learnt this activity from John Morgan.

## 6.14

**MATERIALS**
None

**TRAINEES**
Trainees who have
done some
teaching

# TEACHER GESTURE CIRCLE

## Procedure

1 Everyone stands in a circle.
2 Start off by stepping, just slightly, into the circle and doing a short mime of a typical gesture that you tend to use a lot in class. This could perhaps be wagging a finger, or peering over your glasses, or making a conductor-like wave of your arms to begin a choral drill, or turning towards a reference book and miming yourself searching frantically through its pages. You can accompany your gesture/mime with a sound or a very few words. It is, thus, a presentation to the group, of something you, as a teacher, typically do with a class.
3 All the others in the circle then copy your mime, as exactly as they can and all at the same time.
4 Next, each participant thinks of a gesture that would be typical of herself and then, one by one, participants step into the circle and mime a teaching gesture of their own.
5 After each mime, the group copies the mime.

### VARIATIONS

a Instead of copying the gesture *exactly*, trainees often do it with a little more zest and flair than the original. You can encourage or discourage this yourself by the amount *you* exaggerate when you copy.
b Instead of stepping in with a gesture, trainees can step in with a typical phrase from their own repertoire, for example, praising, starting, stopping, or correcting students.
c A warm-up to this idea is for people to mime typical gestures of other professions such as 'waiter', 'priest', 'fire-fighter', 'politician' and so on.

### RATIONALE/COMMENT

a In this 'mime and mirror' process trainees become more aware of their own habitual teaching gestures (or phrases) by looking at the group copying, and so seeing what these look like (or sound like) from the outside.
b Participants have the chance to learn about each other in a new way and to mirror or shadow others.

ACKNOWLEDGEMENT
I learnt this from Bernard Dufeu.

# CRYSTAL BALL: GUESSING ABOUT OTHERS

## Procedure

1 Participants sit in a circle.
2 Invite the participants to imagine that there is a crystal ball in the centre of the circle. It's an unusual one though. It does not help people to look into the future. It helps people to know, just from looking at someone, what they are like.
3 Someone volunteers to be the first to simply sit and say nothing! Other members of the group look at them and say what they imagine the person is like, what she likes or dislikes, what teaching habits she has, what sort of students she likes best, and so on. All comments start with 'You are . . .', 'You like . . .', 'You dislike . . .' or 'I think you . . .'
4 When the flow of comments seems to be slowing down, announce 'Only thirty seconds more!' This usually brings a flurry of last-minute guesses. Then call 'Time!'
5 The volunteer now says what was true and what wasn't, and also says whether the overall portrait was close to the truth or not.

### RATIONALE/COMMENT

It is rare for people to have the chance to learn, in a structured, sympathetic setting, about the impression they give just from their appearance. As a teacher enters a room of new students, the students will be guessing and projecting, just as colleagues do in this activity. It is thus a good way of finding out what strengths and weaknesses you have simply in your presence before you teach anything.

ACKNOWLEDGEMENT
I learnt this idea from Bernard Dufeu. (See Dufeu, forthcoming.)

### 6.15

**MATERIALS**
None

**TRAINEES**
Ones who have never met before

**TRAINER**
Experienced, flexible, sensitive and with some counselling skills

# SPARE CHANGE OR GIVING AND GETTING

## Procedure

1 Ask trainees to take out of their purses or wallets as much money as they can afford to lose and to hold it visibly in their hands.
2 One by one the participants silently get up and give as much money as they like to whoever they want.
3 Afterwards, one by one, people tell the group how much they got and how they felt about it. People may wish to say how the denominations they took from their pockets made a difference to their decisions. That is, having one five pound note means only being able to give to one person unless you tear the note into pieces. Having a lot of individual coins means you can give to one or many different people.
4 Next, people stand up and, again silently and one by one, take as much money as they want from whoever they want.
5 Everyone counts how much they have now.
6 Again people say how they feel about what they have.

### 6.16

**MATERIALS**
Trainees need their purses/wallets with whatever money is inside

**TRAINEES**
Any

**TRAINER**
Experienced, flexible, sensitive

**RATIONALE/COMMENT**

This dynamic giving and getting process leads into (usually *very* heated) exchanges on free will, social constraint, fairness, taking what you want, receiving, wanting to give, favouritism, and many other issues. Since teachers may be 'givers' or 'withholders', it is an interesting exercise for this professional group. It works well with counsellers, social workers, therapists and business people too.

**VARIATIONS**

I imagine the process would work with other tokens, such as buttons, although I think it might lose some of its power.

ACKNOWLEDGEMENT

I learnt this from Gerlinde Wilberg, who learnt it on a Relate training weekend for marriage guidance counsellors.

## 6.17

**MATERIALS**
None

**TRAINEES**
Any

# LEARNING DIARIES

## Preparation

Look through some of the books mentioned at the end of this activity to familiarise yourself with a wide range of possibilities in diary writing.

## Procedure

1 Introduce participants to the idea of keeping a learning diary. Discuss possible entry headings, types of entry, timing, materials, writing styles, etc.
2 Negotiate with trainees whether they would like to keep their diaries private or would allow others to read some of their writing.
3 Some participants may take up the idea, especially if you provide time *within the timetable* for them to do their thinking and writing.
4 Diaries can remain private. Alternatively, participants – in pairs, small groups or plenary – can share their diaries by reading bits out loud. Individual diarists can decide how much they want to share. While sharing is going on, listeners refrain from commenting or asking questions, and just listen as well as possible.

**VARIATIONS**

a Diaries can be started on particular themes (e.g. 'How I feel in my training group', 'The amount of preparation I do for my classes versus its apparent effectiveness', 'One learner in my class') or this can be left more open.
b Trainees can write diaries in the form of comments to themselves, dialogue or letters to others.
c Participants can show 'open' diaries to the trainer, who reads them and adds comments, questions, suggestions and so on. See Haill (1990). Here, I'm assuming that the trainer does not assess the diary

in any way. If you find that your judgment of trainees *is* affected even by just reading their diaries (that is, reading without formal assessment), then you may like to stop looking at them altogether.

d Trainees can keep their diaries and read them again when they, in turn, are teaching a class. They may find it easier to empathise with their students when reminded of their own feelings when they were undergoing training.

### RATIONALE/COMMENTS

Training courses can be very hectic and social. Diary writing can give participants a chance to react to the course privately and in their own time, and to commit their views to paper – thus using a different channel from discussion and listening. Diaries also form an interesting record of how people felt being students again.

### ACKNOWLEDGEMENTS/READING

A number of people reminded me of the usefulness of diaries in the same few weeks – Chris Sion, Mario Rinvolucri and Ian McGrath and, earlier, Eric Rankin.

Haill (1990), Plomer (1977), Anaïs Nin's *Journals* (any volume), Progoff (1978).

# INNER VOICE

## Procedure

**6.18**

**MATERIALS**
None

**TRAINEES**
Any

1 Tell the trainees that this activity is based on the idea of mental rehearsal or talking to yourself. That is, while having a bath, waiting in a queue, walking to a class, listening to music, sitting in a traffic jam, or anywhere else you have the odd moment, you can, mentally, do any of the following:

- try to remember all your classmates' names,
- go over a lesson plan,
- remember a time when you felt good in your last class,
- imagine starting your class,
- try to remember how people greet each other in your staffroom,
- rehearse what you'll do and say if you can't find your place on the tape or if there's a power cut
- imagine all your students dancing, all in different ways,
- repeat the main points of the syllabus of your training course,
- prepare a joke to tell people,
- go over new terminology, its spelling and meaning,
- imagine miming the difference between 'stumble' and 'stagger',
- go over the main points of a lecture and prepare some questions to ask the trainer about points you didn't understand,
- imagine yourself having tremendous rapport with your next class,

. . . and so on. All this is done silently, in a kind of conversation with yourself, in your imagination.

2 Remind your trainees that this is a useful tool for previewing and reviewing material, for learning, for preparing questions, and for finding out what they do or don't know about something. Create space and time, *in class*, for them to wander around thinking, mumbling or even chanting. You can also set this as part of a coffee-break activity, or as homework, and refer back to it at the start of the next session by asking participants what they have 'inner voiced' since the time before and what they have discovered that they don't understand but need to know.

### RATIONALE/COMMENT
a 'Inner voicing' allows people a measure of solitude in the group.
b It enables people to make use of time that would otherwise be wasted in waiting or feeling frustrated.
c It introduces a technique that participants can encourage their own language students to use in the target language.
d It builds on natural tendencies of mental rehearsal and conversing.

### ACKNOWLEDGEMENT/READING
I first experienced *Inner voice* in French in a workshop given by Chris Sion at the 1987 SEAL Conference.

## 6.19

**MATERIALS**
None

**TRAINEES**
In-service

# STAFFROOM VIDEO

## Procedure

1 Ask trainees to sit comfortably, shut their eyes and run a video in their mind's eye of their staffroom. Encourage them to let their internal/mental video camera roam around the staffroom picking out a person here and a person there.
2 Next, ask them to pick out, again in their mind's eye, someone they know well, to hold the 'camera' on them for a while, and then to freeze the frame.
3 Ask them to open to open their eyes, turn to their neighbour and explain who they saw, what the person was doing, and why they feel they know that person so well.
4 After the pairs have had enough time to share their videos, ask everyone to close their eyes again and let the video camera run again. This time they let it roam around the staffroom until it picks out someone more in the shadows, someone less well-known. Then, they freeze the frame again.
5 Again they open their eyes, turn to their neighbour and say who they saw, what this person was doing, and why they feel that they don't know that person very well. The neighbour tries to give suggestions of possible ways to get to know that person better.

## VARIATIONS

You can use the same basic process to encourage trainees to visualise, for example, their own board work, an idyllic classroom, a student who is troubling them, a favourite student, their classroom and students just before they, the teacher, come in or just after they leave.

## RATIONALE/COMMENT

**a** Often, in a staffroom with low staff turnover, cliques form. Some people get on well together, but find channels to other people in the same staffroom completely blocked. This exercise makes individual teachers more aware of who they do and don't relate to well.

**b** It also helps people to get started on thinking about how they might be able to unblock channels of communication. It can help to integrate new, shy or quiet staff. It can create an atmosphere of 'thaw' rather than the acceptance of frozen relationships.

ACKNOWLEDGEMENT
I learnt this from Natalie Hess in 1989.


# VALUES CLARIFICATION

## Procedure

**6.20**

**MATERIALS**
Situation worksheets and discussion worksheets (examples below)

**TRAINEES**
Any

1 Invite trainees to read a situation worksheet (see the example below) which recounts a story of moral issues with several characters included.
2 Once the trainees have read the situation worksheet, they work individually at ranking the characters in the situation from 1 ('least objectionable') to 6 ('most objectionable'). Meanwhile, write up on the board the names of all the characters involved. In the situation below they are Vera, Mick, Don, Angie, Rachel and Peter.
3 On completion of the individual ranking, ask participants to form small groups and try to reach a consensus about the ranking.
4 Each group presents its ranking to other groups. This can be done orally by group representatives speaking one by one in plenary or by different groups displaying lists or posters.
5 Finish with open plenary discussion. If necessary, prompt this by using a discussion sheet such as the example below.

## VARIATIONS

**a** Situations can highlight any moral issue in teaching and learning, for instance, relationships with students, discipline, sexist and racist materials, union membership, cheating in exams, the presence of management at training sessions, the lack of women on selection committees, or any other issue relevant to your situation.

**b** Ask participants who have recently encountered a moral issue at work if they would like to write up situation sheets.

c Assign reading on ways of handling conflict, for example, TET (Teacher Effectiveness Training, see below), before or after the session.

### RATIONALE/COMMENT

a Many people coming into TEFL have not worked with adults or children in multinational classes, with people from different cultures than their own, with people generally, or have never been in a position of (some) authority or power before. Thorough preparation for teaching, then, should include opportunities to define and refine value systems.

b It is relatively rare for practising teachers to have the chance to discuss a moral issue without the issue and the discussion being directly relevant to someone they are involved with. Values clarification activities provide an opportunity to do so.

### ACKNOWLEDGEMENT/READING

I learnt about values clarification activities from Mike Lavery (Lavery 1988).

### Situation worksheet for white teachers working with multiracial groups

Vera is the main teacher of an advanced group of language learners. She swaps for one period a day with Mick, a white American teacher, who is very interested in literature. Vera doesn't feel she knows much about literature and so she is happy to let Mick take full responsibility for the preparation, materials and homework that he does with her class.

On teaching her own class again, after a swapped lesson and at the end of the day, Vera finds a handout of a poem lying on a desk. The poem is called 'Niggers'. It has apparently been given out to everyone in the class. Vera notices it as most students have left the room. She checks with one student, Don, and he says the poem had 'a good attitude'.

The next day Angie, the only black student in the class, looks detached during the first lesson and, as Vera leaves her class again to swap into Mick's class, Angie leaves the room too. Vera asks her if she's feeling unwell. Angie says, 'I don't appreciate Mick. I don't want to stay. Are you teaching us again this afternoon?' Vera replies, 'Yes.' 'Then I'll see you later', says Angie. She walks off across campus towards the library.

In the lunch break Vera meets Mick in the staffroom to talk about the incident. 'The poem is just a period piece', says Mick. 'It just illustrates attitudes in the South at the turn of the century. It's history.' Another teacher, Rachel, overhearing the conversation says, 'I don't think you should use anything political in the classroom. It's just asking for trouble.' Another teacher, Peter, says, 'You can't have students walking out every time they don't happen to like a text. They're here to learn English, not have chips on their shoulders. You should penalise Angie for absenteeism.' Vera looks astonished. To her, the incident proves that white people can be totally insensitive to systemic racism.

© Longman Group UK Ltd 1992

Discussion sheet

1 Which experience from your past did the story bring to mind?
2 How was your ranking related to any differences between your personal and professional values? What choices did you have to make?
3 What similarities and differences arose among the members of your group?
4 What issues seemed most important to your group?
5 How did value conflicts within your group affect the consensus process? Was conflict over values resolved? If so, how?
6 What did this experience show you about your own values and individual values generally?
7 What can you infer from this exercise about the consistency of personal values with those expressed by colleagues or organisations?
8 What are some ways of negotiating value conflicts in *organisations*?

© Longman Group UK Ltd 1992

# STATEMENT MODIFICATION
## Procedure

1 At dictation speed, read out a list of statements connected with an area of teaching or learning such as the use of dictionaries in language classes, for example:
- Dictionaries should be banned from the language classroom.
- Students should spend one class hour a week on dictionary work.
- When students use dictionaries in class, it shows that I have failed to explain a word properly.
- When students use dictionaries in class, they cannot concentrate on what I'm saying.
- I feel more secure if all the dictionaries in class are on *my* desk.
- It is essential that students learn to use dictionaries well.
- My greatest concern is that students should use a monolingual rather than a bilingual dictionary.
- I find dictionaries quite complicated myself and I hardly ever use them.
- Dictionaries are essential. I don't speak English well enough to help students with all the vocabulary they need.
- If all new vocabulary is pretaught carefully, there's no real need for dictionaries in class.
- I'd feel happier if all the students had the same dictionary and preferably changed it when they change from Elementary to Intermediate and from Intermediate to Advanced.
- I can't speak any other language well enough to check if what students find in a bilingual dictionary is correct.
- I am still using the same bilingual dictionary I had when I was an intermediate student.

## 6.21

**MATERIALS**
One copy of some statements about the topic of the session

**TRAINEES**
Any

**2** Trainees write these statements down one by one in their notebooks, but edit them mentally first. That is, they keep any part of a statement they want to and change any part they wish. Thus, the first statement above could be written down like this:

- Dictionaries shouldn't be banned from any classroom.
  or like this:
- Bad dictionaries with old-fashioned examples should be banned from schools.

The way trainees write a sentence down depends on their views. If they completely agree with the original statement, then they write it down exactly as it is in the original.

**3** The participants then discuss the statements and the changes they made with a neighbour, in small groups or in the whole group.

**VARIATIONS**

**a** The statements can be about any area of teaching or learning, for example: whether students should be allowed to be silent during the early days of a course, whether drills are a good idea, whether correction is necessary, whether rote learning is a good technique, etc.

**b** The statements can be given out as a list to trainees who can modify them at home.

**RATIONALE/COMMENT**

**a** Reacting to other peoples' statements by changing them in detail, in part or completely, according to your own opinions, makes you feel powerful. A statement, once modified, can be modified again. Opinions seem to be less rigid once you have crossed out or rephrased words on a page.

**b** Again, it is valuable to discover the range of views represented within the group on any topic.

ACKNOWLEDGEMENT/READING

I discovered statement modification for myself during a dictation (that I disagreed with) given by Gerry Kenny on an orientation course. On mentioning my modifications to others, I discovered that I had reinvented an old, well-known technique.

## PARALLEL LEARNING
### Procedure

1 Ask how many trainees are learning something not connected with EFL, such as word processing, cooking, car maintenance, a language or gardening.
2 If only a few people are learning anything, try to lay on opportunities for language classes or informal ten-minute sessions on how to juggle or any other subject that someone can teach in the institution where your course is being run.
3 After one or more trainees have undergone a learning session outside or parallel to the course, invite them to write down, individually, some of their reactions to and feelings about the subject, the learning, the teacher, the process or anything else they wish.
4 Allow time for individuals to share anything they want to from their writing with other colleagues.
5 Invite trainees to say what they have learned about themselves as learners or teachers.

### RATIONALE/COMMENT

a This process accepts that people have interesting lives outside their training courses and that these lives can be useful and relevant to the training/learning process.
b Writing things down individually means that private space is made where individuals can reflect and commit themselves to a point of view without being swayed by others in the group.
c The activity draws attention to the similarities between various teaching/learning experiences rather than the differences.

READING
Cranmer (1988).

**6.22**

MATERIALS
None

TRAINEES
Any

# Section 2: Finding out about the job

In many senses, everyone who has ever gone to school knows what teaching and teachers are all about. However, reflection time and encouragement may be necessary for this knowledge to become conscious and expressible. One way of learning what it would be like to be a teacher would be to 'follow' a teacher through their day, watching what they do, asking them about their decisions and options, talking to their students and helping out. If this kind of informal apprenticeship is not possible, then pre-service trainees will have to commit time, money and energy to a training course on the off-chance of finding that they turn out to be capable of doing the job and enjoying it. The ideas in this section may help to bring out some of the issues involved in teaching. 6.20 *Values clarification* could be useful here too.

## 6.23

**MATERIALS**
Several copies of a list, enough sticky labels (or labels with pins) for each participant

**TRAINEES**
Any

# THE FLEXIBLE LIST

## Preparation

1 Draw up a numbered list of, for example, some of the qualities or needs of a teacher. The list should be about twenty items long. The last item should be 'Something else' followed by a space for things you haven't thought of.
2 Make a few copies of the list and pin them up at different points in the room.

## Procedure

1 Give everyone a label.
2 Explain that all the lists are the same. Ask the participants to go and read one of them, choose two qualities or needs that they agree with, and write the numbers that go with these qualities on their label. So, for example, if the list starts like this:

Needs/Qualities of a teacher

1 Organisational ability
2 Respect for authority
3 Desire to educate people
4 Free weekends
5 Posh clothing

and if the trainee agrees that items (1) and (4) are necessary to make someone a good teacher, then they write 1 and 4 on their label. If a trainee can find nothing on the list to agree with, they can write out a new quality or two, both on their label and at the bottom of the list.
3 The trainees then pin their labels on themselves and mill around looking at other people's labels. They try to find someone who has one number in common with them. When they do, they stop and discuss why they both think the corresponding quality or need is important.
4 Next, trainees mill around looking for people who share neither of their numbers. They discuss their differences of opinion.
5 Next, they go back to the list to find the 'neglected third child', that is, the idea on the list that they would have liked to have chosen but couldn't because they could only choose two items. They then sit down in threes and discuss these last choices.

**VARIATIONS**
a The list can be a list of anything, for example, different learning styles, what makes a good student, a principal's roles, or different types of correction policy.
b It can be drawn up by individuals, groups or the trainer.
c Draw up a list for a particular area of input and use it before input or discussion and then again afterwards to see how trainees have or have not changed in their thinking as a result of a session or course.

**RATIONALE/COMMENT**

a Choosing from and adding to the list helps people to clarify their own thoughts and priorities.

b The process of discussing, comparing and contrasting views with others further clarifies where trainees stand in relation to each other and is a useful way to lead in to a subject.

c The process has a nice mixture of structure and relaxed conversation.

ACKNOWLEDGEMENT/READING
I learnt this from Natalie Hess. See Hess (1989).

# WHAT'S IT LIKE BEING A TEACHER?

## Procedure

1 Find enough practising teachers who are willing to be interviewed so that each trainee or each pair of trainees has the opportunity to conduct an interview.

2 Explain to trainees that they will be interviewing experienced teachers. Before participants contact the teachers (you can do the matching up), they spend time working on interview techniques. There should be discussion on how to structure conversations, how to listen well, prompt gently and show interest, how to respect privacy, how to create a good atmosphere, which questions are OK, not OK and so on.

3 Discuss a possible interview structure, for example (a) fact questions, (b) opinion questions, (c) analytical questions, and (d) probing questions (see examples below).

Trainees work in groups to build their side of the interviews. Questions range from ones about salaries and pension rights to those about the frustrations and satisfactions of the work as well as questions about educational philosophy.

N.B. It is important that the teachers interviewed know that there will be a discussion of their replies on the training course later.

4 Give trainees a deadline by which to complete their interviews.

5 Trainees bring the results to class and discuss what they have learnt about the job and the people who do it.

**VARIATIONS**

a The topic of the interview can be narrowly focused on, for example, handling discipline problems or avoiding teacher burn-out.

b Interviews can be conducted by letter, phone or audio cassette.

c Interviewees can choose what questions they want to answer.

d Trainees can interview each other, the trainer, new teachers or retired ones.

**6.24**

**MATERIALS**
None

**TRAINEES**
Pre-service

**REQUIREMENT**
Access to experienced teachers

### RATIONALE/COMMENT

**a** Trainees are introduced to the culture of teaching by personal contact with practising teachers, perhaps for the first time since their own schooldays. They begin to deepen their acquaintance with the problems, responsibilites and human interest of the teacher's world.

**b** Much of the discussion on listening well, creating a good atmosphere and so forth applies equally to teaching.

**c** Provided people are approached sensitively, the interviews can give interviewees a chance to clarify their own thoughts about their work. It may also help them to realise that their own experience is valuable to others.

### ACKNOWLEDGEMENT/READING

I learnt this idea from Natalie Hess. See Hess (1987).

Example questions

*Fact questions*

1 How long have you been a teacher?

2 Could you describe the school where you teach?

*Opinion questions*

1 What was the most and what was the least helpful to you in your professional training?

2 What are some satisfactions and frustrations of your work?

*Analytical questions*

1 What, in your opinion, is the most difficult aspect of teaching?

2 Can you compare teaching to any other profession?

*Probing questions*

1 Could you describe a difficult professional situation and tell me how you coped with it?

2 Has teaching changed your personality?

© Longman Group UK Ltd 1992

## 6.25

**MATERIALS**
None

**TRAINEES**
In-sevice; this process may work best with trainees who are being trained away from their own institutions

## CASE STUDIES

### Procedure

1 Ask each trainee to work on a case study of either a student, a staffroom, a school hierarchy or a class. You can give out the topic of the case study or ask trainees to choose one.

2 Trainees gather information by observing, reading, interviewing or other means. They can work individually or in pairs or groups.

3 Participants can write up their studies for presentation in a variety of formats, for example, as a sociogram (see Figure 25), an organigram (see Figure 26), a route map (see page 166), a report, an essay, a diary, a poster, a tape recording, etc.

**a** The sociogram
This diagram consists of concentric circles. The protagonist
(perhaps the trainee, perhaps a student in her class) puts her own
name in the centre. The protagonist adds names, on the inner rings,
of people in the class/school she is closest to. The names of people
she relates to less closely are plotted on the outer rings, as in
Figure 25.

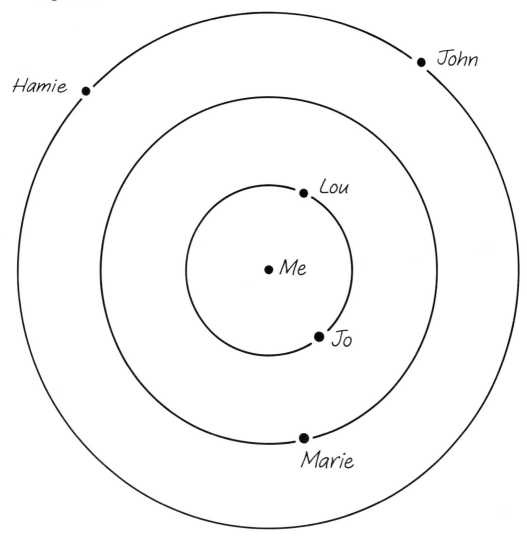

Fig. 25 The sociogram

**b** The organigram
This diagram is like a family tree, but instead of having relatives'
names on it, it shows the hierarchical structure of an organisation,
as in Figure 26 overleaf.

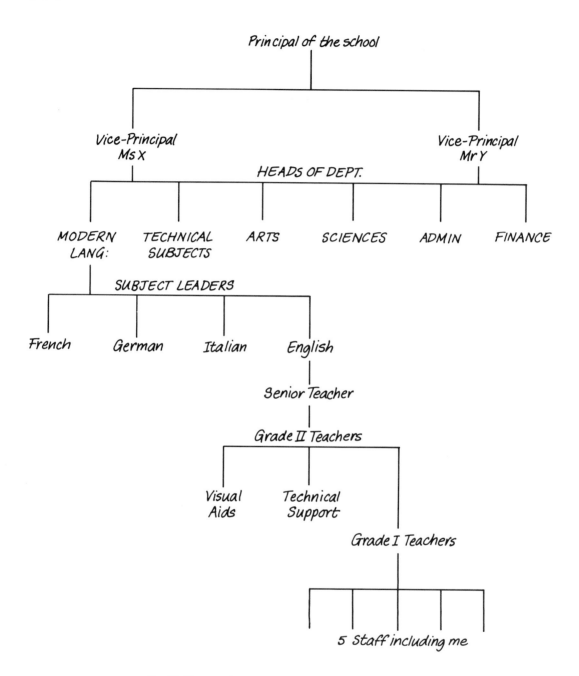

Fig. 26 The organigram

**c** The route map
Trainees each make a diagram of their work area, showing tables, chairs, windows and so forth. Each participant draws a dotted line to show their usual paths during a work session. Once completed, the diagrams usually show up much-used and no-go areas. Badly-organised and crowded areas may also come to light.

**VARIATIONS**

**a** All participants work on the same topic or different individuals work on different topics.

**b** Case studies can be presented one by one in consecutive sessions, all in the same session or swapped and taken home for private listening, reading and comment. In this last case, they are part of the course 'library', along with copies of trainees' assignments, lesson plans and materials that can be kept in a lockable cupboard or in a cardboard box in the training room.

**c** This approach to case studies allows and encourages people to find out in detail about something that interests them and to represent these findings in whatever form best suits their expressive flair.

ACKNOWLEDGEMENT/READING
Open University (1979), Hulbert (1986) and Jordan (1983).

# LEFT TO RIGHT DIALOGUE

## Procedure

**6.26**

**MATERIALS**
None

**TRAINEES**
Any

1 All the trainees sit round a table each with a sheet of paper in front of them.

2 Ask them to relax and just listen to the situation you are going to describe. You might say, for example:

'Imagine that you're in class. You've prepared your lesson well and are actually quite looking forward to teaching it. Since the beginning of term, though, one student has been looking a bit bored. She's been yawning, leaning back and shuffling around in her seat. In this lesson, you've asked her, by name, a couple of questions about the work, to help her to get involved in it, but it hasn't worked. She keeps shuffling in her bag and looking out of the window. Other students around her are getting distracted. She keeps whispering to her colleagues and you find that really distracting. She asks if she can leave the room for a while, and while she's out there's peace and quiet. It doesn't last long though. She's soon back, walking *very* noisily to her seat. She sits down with a huge sigh and starts talking to her neighbour in more than a whisper. About four or five people around her are now thoroughly distracted.'

3 After talking them through a situation such as this, ask the trainees to take their sheets of paper and write *Teacher:* ' at the top left of the page. The inverted comma shows the start of a dialogue. Then the trainees write down exactly what they would say, if they were the teacher, in this situation.

4 Everyone now passes their paper to the person on their left. On receiving the new sheet of paper from their right, everyone writes *Student* ' underneath what the previous trainee has written. They then continue with what they think the student's response would be to the opening remark.

5 Once everybody has written the student's line of dialogue, the papers are passed back to the person on the right. The person who started off the teacher's part in the dialogue now writes the teacher's next remark in response to the student's.

6 The activity continues, with each participant involved in the two different written role plays. Give plenty of time for people to think and write. Make sure all paper moving takes place at the same time.

7 After fifteen to twenty minutes, ask trainees to stick their dialogues up on the walls so that everyone can read them.

8 People discuss how they feel about the way their conversations developed.

**VARIATIONS**

a Use other situations involving two main protagonists who may come into conflict, for example, a teacher telling a student they have failed a course or a teacher asking for help with a class.

b Trainees can write one side of the dialogue with their left and the other with their right hands. Try asking people to write the normally more powerful role with their weaker writing hand.

c This idea also works well in the training of trainers too. For example, trainers can have left-right dialogues about giving and receiving feedback after an observed lesson.

**RATIONALE/COMMENT**

This written, double role play enables one person to experience both roles in a situation and to have two very different kinds of conversation depending on the content and tenor of the opening remarks. Discussion can follow on methods of resolving conflict as well as on useful and useless conversation patterns with students.

ACKNOWLEDGEMENT/READING

I learnt this from Mario Rinvolucri as an idea for use in the language classroom. See Frank and Rinvolucri (1983 p. 119). And, about handling conflicts in the classroom, Gordon (1974).

## 6.27

**MATERIALS**
Copies of job advertisements and, if possible, job descriptions for jobs within the field

**TRAINEES**
Pre-service

# PLOTTING PRIORITIES

## Preparation

1 Towards the end of a course ask your trainees to write down, for homework, one list entitled 'What I think my trainers think are the most important qualities a teacher should have' and another list entitled 'What *I* think are the most important qualities to develop in myself as a teacher'. Ask them to put at least five, preferably more, points under each heading and to bring their lists to the next session.

2 You prepare a list too, entitled 'The most important qualities I'd like trainees to develop as teachers'.

## Procedure

1 Each trainee reads out their first list to the whole group. Listen and then read out your own list. Discussion follows.

2 Next, participants pair up and discuss their second lists. While they are doing this, pin up job advertisements and job descriptions for EFL teaching posts. You can cull these from *EFL Gazette, The Guardian* (Tuesday), *The Times Educational Supplement, TESOL Newsletter*, local papers, British Council circulars, or whatever are the main sources of job advertisements in your situation.

3 When everyone has finished discussing their own lists, invite them to stand up, move around, and read the advertisements and job descriptions.

4 After reading, ask them to make a third list entitled, 'What employers seem to think are the most important qualities in an employable language teacher'.

5 Discussion follows.

### RATIONALE/COMMENT

a This is a useful decompression process at the end of an intensive, assessed course. It establishes priorities and helps people to return to the 'real' world again.

b It may create a chance for trainees and trainers to evaluate the relevance of their work on the course, to discuss adaptations to things learnt, or to adapt the course!

## WHAT AREAS OF LANGUAGE DO I NEED TO BE AWARE OF?

## Procedure

### SESSION 1

1 Give out copies of a worksheet such as the one below. Ask trainees to read through the worksheet. Give them examples of each of the language categories mentioned.

2 Ask them to keep the worksheet by them while attending lectures, reading, observing classes (live or on video), practice teaching, during their free time, in fact, *all* the time! Ask them to note down *verbatim* examples for whichever category they prefer and to bring them to the next session along with a note of where each example was collected.

### SESSION TWO

3 Ask the trainees to read out the examples of language they have collected.

4 Discuss whatever these examples throw up.

## 6.28

**MATERIALS**
A class set of a worksheet (see below)

**TRAINEES**
Pre-service

**SESSIONS**
Two

### VARIATION

Split the list on the worksheet below into, say, four separate sheets with different items on. Give each trainee one sheet. Then, in the next session, ask trainees with the same sheets to discuss in groups of four the examples they've collected. Trainees copy down interesting examples collected by others in the group. Then get trainees to form new groups of four where every trainee has a different sheet along with their own (by now probably lengthened) list of examples.

### RATIONALE/COMMENT

Both native and non-native speaking pre-service trainees will need help to become aware of the different categories of language discussed or used in language teaching. Making them collect data for themselves rather than presenting it to them in lecture or handout form encourages them to rely on their own resources and on real usage rather than on standard works of reference or inauthentic examples in coursebooks. It prepares them for an approach to language work that rests on real data, and on real usage, rather than on prescriptive rules.

### ACKNOWLEDGEMENTS

Thanks to John Morgan and Peter Grundy for comment on this activity.

#### Language categories worksheet

Collect a few authentic examples of each of the following categories of language; note the situation of use for each.

a Language specific to the field of EFL, i.e. terminology from linguistics and methodology met in lectures, staffrooms, resource books and at conferences.

b Language a teacher uses in the classroom to set up pairwork, stop groupwork, attract attention, etc. that is, class management language.

c Natural spoken language. Take it down verbatim as faithfully as you can. Do not translate or omit the slips, hesitations, and non-grammatical but meaningful items you hear.

d Language that you want to present to your students.

e Language found in songs, poems and prose literature that reflects cultural attitudes/factors.

f Any language that reflects any cultural attitude whatsoever.

g Language that students use to stop the teacher and ask questions in class.

h Interaction language that students use with each other when settling into an activity. These items may well be in the mother tongue unless known in the target language.

i Language rules that you were taught were correct when you were at school, together with language heard or read in real use that seems to contradict these rules.

j Unnatural adjustments in a teacher's own language when the teacher is talking to elementary and intermediate language students.

k Acceptable but different ways of saying the same thing in different regions of the English-speaking world.

© Longman Group UK Ltd 1992

# CHAPTER 7

# *Support*

For many – even those really looking forward to a training or learning event – stepping back into the role of learner, sitting down behind a desk again, suffering being told what to do, facing deadlines, creating work that is judged by others, all these things, are stressful. Quite suddenly a person who felt competent and confident before they came to the event can feel de-skilled, nervous, unsure or angry. Many of the processes in this book are aimed at ensuring dignity and balance within training relationships. The processes in this chapter focus particularly on providing support from peer to peer, person to person. This is the rationale behind all of them. It is indicative, I'm afraid, of my own lack of art, and perhaps also of the state of training generally, that this is the slimmest chapter in the book. My own aim for the future is to gain more ways of decreasing the stress of training.

## PAIR CONTRACTS: TALKING AND LISTENING

### Procedure

1 Ask people to sit in pairs near someone they feel comfortable with. Tell them they will be talking to each other about, for example, a strength and a weakness in their own teaching. They will need to be non-judgmental in look, gesture and voice at every stage of the activity.

**7.1**

**MATERIALS**
None

**TRAINEES**
Any

**2** Before they start talking, the pairs make contracts about how much time they want to give to each other (e.g. five or ten minutes each) and to discuss how honest they think they might like to be (e.g. 60%, 90%, 100%).

**3** Person A goes first and talks about something she feels about her class, her teaching techniques, the course or herself. B listens as well as possible and does not interrupt at all. When A has finished, B can ask *factual* questions only. Time-keeping must be exact. If the pair has contracted to give each other five minutes, then A must stop or be stopped after *exactly* five minutes. A can state whether she would like B to offer any possible solutions or comments at this stage or not. Neither A nor B should make any judgments about either the initial outpouring, the problem or the solution.

**4** Next it is B's chance to talk for the agreed time and for A to listen well. Again, after B has stopped talking, A can ask factual questions. B can state whether she would like any ideas, solutions or advice. Neither participant judges either the initial talk or the response.

**5** Before repeating the exercise, either on the same day or on a different day, you need to remind people that it is (a) perfectly natural for some people to hit it off at once and others not to hit it off at all, and (b) that it is OK to change partners or to stay with the same partner as before. Those who choose to stay together can deepen their understanding of each other. Those who change may note a difference of approach between the different partners they work with. It is important for partners to negotiate the length of talking time and the degree of honesty and to make a contract on both these points *every time* before starting this process.

**6** The chances are strong that, if a pair has worked well together during a formal session, they will try this process outside course time too.

ACKNOWLEDGEMENT/READING
Thanks to Jenny Hoadley for spending a morning telling me about her co-counselling experiences. See Heron (1974).

## 7.2

**MATERIALS**
None

**TRAINEES**
Any

# HEADACHE/ASPIRIN

## Procedure

**1** Give time for participants to come up with one problem they have in their teaching careers. If a few people say they have no problems, don't force them to have one!

**2** Pair people up. One partner in each pair is 'Headache' and the other is 'Aspirin'.

**3** 'Headache' starts by stating her problem. 'Aspirin' just listens as carefully as possible. Then, 'Aspirin' offers one possible solution to the problem, starting with the words, 'You might try . . .' 'Headache' just listens. No judgmental comments are allowed.

4 Then 'Headache' and 'Aspirin' swap roles. When they have finished, they change partners (but each keeps their same 'headache') until they have had several 'aspirins'.

### VARIATION

Have one 'Headache' person and five 'Aspirin' people. 'Headache' does not explain what the problem is. 'Aspirins' start giving advice to which 'Headache' responds. From the responses the 'Aspirins' try to work out what the problem is.

### RATIONALE/COMMENT

a Trainees have a chance to talk about their problems without interruption.

b Solutions are offered that may or may not work, but the solutions are not blocked or judged.

c Solutions are found from within the group.

### ACKNOWLEDGEMENT

I learnt this from Natalie Hess. The variation comes from Gerry Kenny.


# THE RESOURCES BOX

## Procedure

**7.3**

**MATERIALS**
A large cardboard box

**TRAINEES**
Trainees who are actually teaching and sometimes need workable ideas fast or who want to go beyond or away from the set reading

1 Show the box to the trainees and store it in a place where they often gather.

2 The idea is that if anyone comes across an interesting piece of reading, a cartoon, a teaching idea, a reading list and so forth that they think other people in the group might be interested in, they put one copy of it in the box. They write the name of the contribution in a notebook that is kept near the box. They add their name by the new entry in the book too.

3 Anyone can borrow anything they like from the box on the principle that 'If you are a person who likes to take things out of the box, then put some things in too sometimes.' It's a good idea for people to sign their names in the book if they want to borrow something for a long time. That way, others can trace the contribution if they need to.

### VARIATION

The box can act as a notice/conversation/message board.

### ACKNOWLEDGEMENT

At a time when all the materials at the school were being tidied up, weeded out, classified and catalogued, the staff at a school I once worked at decided to institute 'the box' as an anarchic and transient form of sharing.

## 7.4

**MATERIALS**
None

**TRAINEES**
Any, although one variation involves pairing different kinds of trainees

# HELPING PAIRS
## Procedure

1 Each trainee selects a partner.
2 Partners decide how often they will meet, where and for how long.
3 They discuss the form and aims of the meetings, for example:
   - to assess their goals and their achievement of them,
   - to review, recall and learn course material,
   - to tell each other of changes they want to make or risks they want to take and to say whether they managed to make or take them,
   - to interview each other.
4 Partners decide to meet until they wish to stop or decide *definitely* to continue until the end of the course.

**VARIATIONS**
**a** Either you or the trainees can set the aims of the meetings.
**b** After a number of meetings, the group brainstorms new aims.
**c** Helping pairs can consist of: a more experienced course participant and a newcomer to the profession or to the course, an experienced non-native teacher and an inexperienced native-speaking one, or a language student and a trainee.

**RATIONALE/COMMENT**
This idea acknowledges that learning can take place between participants and builds this informal peer learning into the structure of the course. It can be used deliberately to complement strengths and weaknesses. Thus, for example, pairing an experienced non-native teacher with an inexperienced native speaker forces both to acknowledge that they need each other's strengths.

## 7.5

**MATERIALS**
None

**TRAINEES**
Any just finishing a teacher training course

**TIME OF THE COURSE**
At the end

# A LETTER TO THE NEXT GROUP
## Procedure

1 In the last meeting(s) of a course, ask the group to write a letter to a course participant who is due to attend the *next* course. They can start their letters, 'Dear New Participant' or use real names (e.g. 'Dear Renny') if these are known.
2 Ask everyone to try to remember how they felt on the first day of their course and to think of anything they wish they'd known before they started. Then ask them to write a friendly letter to the new course participants giving any help or advice they think would be useful.
3 The letters can be written at home or in class time. They can be open or sealed. They can be passed on to the new trainees.
4 At the end of the second course, ask your trainees what they thought of the letter they received from the previous group and whether it was helpful or not. Give each the chance to write a letter back to their

correspondent from the previous group telling them how they got on. Alternatively, they write letters to the participants on the next course.

**RATIONALE/COMMENT**

Although this process is initiated by you, the trainer, it can be trainee-centred. One trainee, with children and a not-very-helpful husband, chose to write a letter to all the mothers coming on the next course. She said she wanted to encourage them by saying things like, 'Don't worry if the house is a mess sometimes. Better the house than you, your work or your job in a few months' time!'

ACKNOWLEDGEMENT

I learnt this from Jim Wingate. A similar letter writing idea is also mentioned in Deller (1990).

# A TEAM BUILDING EXERCISE

## Procedure

**7.6**

**MATERIALS**
None

**TRAINEES**
Any on a teacher training course which involves them working in groups

1 Get together a group of trainees who will be studying or working together. You can, of course, join in too.
2 Ask everyone to write down several sentences about two key areas: (1) how well they tackle problems, (2) how well they work with other people in a team. The sentences can start with phrases such as 'I'm good at . . .', 'I'm not good at . . .' or, alternatively, 'I don't know what/if I'm good at . . . but . . .'
3 Ask trainees to read these out and discuss them.
4 Give them a task to do together. (See, for example, 2.19 *Creative workshops,* 2.20 *Discovery work,* 3.2 *Dividing up tasks* and 4.14 *Making a terminology board.*)
5 After the task is finished, allow time for a discussion of whether people were right about themselves when they wrote their statements before the task.

**RATIONALE/COMMENT**

a This process focuses trainees' attention on their own and other people's gifts and talents.
b Trainees can note whether they or others are accurate about their own strengths and weaknesses. I find that we often *believe* we are good or bad at something simply because someone once told us this.
c Trainees find out what strengths are present in the group. This is invaluable information for later on when they may be studying, planning and teaching lessons together as well as observing each other and commenting on each other's lessons.

ACKNOWLEDGEMENT

I learnt this from Gerry Kenny.

## 7.7

**MATERIALS**
None

**PARTICIPANTS**
Working teachers
and retired
colleagues or
trainees from past
and present
courses

# SCANDINAVIAN STAFFROOM
## Procedure

A colleague of mine returned enthusiastic from a trip to Scandinavia telling us of a wonderful system there. When staff had retired, they were invited back to have coffee each morning in the main staffroom at the school they'd been teaching at. The retired staff had a table of their own and so could meet colleagues from their own era. They were invited to come a little early and stay on a little so that they could relax and/or help any working staff who needed ideas. They could help by photocopying or gathering resources or talking over teaching situations. They thus had a place in the school still, the role of helping the busier staff and a chance to meet former colleagues again.

This idea can be adapted for teacher training courses by encouraging past trainees to drop back in to the training centre after their course is over. They can meet each other and meet the trainees, ask any questions they like, and help out any present trainees on the new course with sympathy or practical help and ideas. If your school is pressed for space, try a local café or coffee bar instead of the staffroom.

## 7.8

**MATERIALS**
None

**TRAINEES**
Equal numbers of
inexperienced
trainees who feel
out of touch or lack
confidence, and
experienced,
working teachers

**TIME IN THE
COURSE**
Just before the
course starts or,
alternatively,
instead of a course

**REQUIREMENT**
Working teachers
willing to help

# INFORMAL APPRENTICESHIP
## Preparation

Contact the teachers and work out with them what they are willing to do. For example:

Can the inexperienced person watch the teacher teach? If so, how often and for how long? What rules would the teacher like the apprentice (or intern) to follow as regards joining in or not in class, choosing a place to sit, making notes or not, talking to the teacher before, during and after the lesson? Can the apprentice/intern prepare materials for the teacher, monitor groupwork, lead any warm-up or filler activities, write things on the board, correct homework?

## Procedure

1 Once the teacher has sketched out a plan of involvement, arrange a meeting between you, the teacher and the apprentice where the *teacher* explains what they would like.
2 Arrange, within the teacher's timetable, slots for liaison time. This will mean that the apprenticeship system can happen without undue rush and stress.
3 End apprenticeships when the training course starts (if the relationship has been built up before a course), but allow time in both apprentices' and teachers' schedules for them to get together once in a while to find out how the apprentice, the class and the class teacher are getting on in their new work.

## RATIONALE/COMMENT

**a** For experienced teachers thinking of doing some teacher training, this is a natural and relatively unstressful way of getting some experience. It can also add variety to the normal job of teaching.

**b** The apprentice can help reduce the teacher's workload by helping with materials preparation, photocopying and so on.

**c** If the system happens before a training course, the apprentices start their training course more in touch with current practice.

**d** A relationship is formed between teachers, apprentices and classes which could continue.

**e** The apprentice can compare and contrast what they learn on a course with the reality of the classroom practice as they've recently experienced it.

**f** I first saw this system at work at Hilderstone College, Broadstairs, Kent. It was used for course participants who had less experience, training or confidence than others. Usually only one or two out of a group of ten had had an informal apprenticeship before their course started. The teachers approached about accepting an apprentice were often those who had shown an interest in moving into teacher training.

# WHO NEEDS A CUDDLE TODAY?

## Procedure

**7.9**

**MATERIALS**
None

**TRAINEES**
Any

Everybody has up days and down days. Trainees can have lots of down days, days when they feel they aren't progressing as it's all too much. It's rare on a group course however that *everybody* is equally down on the same day. Those who feel positive can cheer up those who don't.

## Procedure

**1** Ask if there is anybody who is feeling particularly grouchy, fed up or disconsolate and wouldn't mind being cheered up. Don't ask why they are feeling fed up.

**2** Once somebody has owned up (and this happens more readily as people get to know the activity), initiate a brief energy-raising activity for that trainee. Examples of things you can do are:

**a** Start a hearty round of applause for the trainee by clapping in her direction. As the others in the group join in, make your own clapping louder. Whistle, cheer, shout 'She's great!', smile and stamp your feet until the whole group is really loud and active. This not only cheers up the trainee but also raises the group's energy too.

**b** Use the feedback idea in 5.29 *What can I learn from you?*, but just for the 'down' participant.

**c** Get everyone to sing 'For she's a jolly good fellow'.

**d** Get the group to make soothing noises and comments, such as 'Oh!', 'Aaah', 'Poor old Sally', 'Never mind' and 'It'll be OK' – again, at good volume and all at the same time with real sympathy intonation.

**e** Suggest that those who are good at cuddling give the trainee a cuddle (if she wants one!).

**f** Ask everybody to be particularly friendly and nice to the trainee *instantly*. Some people will say, 'You look great!', others, 'Shall I call you at the weekend so we can do the homework together?', and so forth. Someone else might pass her a mint.

**g** Ask the 'down' participant to think of one thing, one small thing, one silly thing even, that the group or people in the group can do to cheer her up. The answer could be, 'Tell a joke, someone' or 'Sing a song' or 'Give me a lift home', etc. Immediately, *everybody* offers to do this *energetically*, all at once. Thus, if the trainee says, 'Tell a joke, someone', then everyone in the room starts a joke (even if they can't think of one) so that the air is full of people saying, 'A funny thing happened to me the other day . . .', 'Have you heard the one about . . .?', 'There was this old lady . . .', 'A friend of mine said . . .', 'There was an Irishwoman, a Scotsman and . . .' and so on. With this sudden burst of incomprehensible energy the participant and the group usually burst out laughing.

**3** Once trainees have done the activity a few times for different 'down' trainees, if you are having a bad day, you too can say that you feel awful and ask for any of the cuddle variations above.

**RATIONALE/COMMENT**

This activity involves accepting that people, including trainers, have off days and involves, as well, doing something simple to improve things.

ACKNOWLEDGEMENT

Mike Gradwell introduced me to the use of applause to raise confidence. If I hadn't experienced it and loved it, I would have thought the idea was both crazy and embarrassing!

# GROUP LIAISON TIME

## Procedure

1 Set aside a regular twenty to forty minute slot for trainees to meet each other as a group, without you being present.
2 Explain that everyone has to turn up for this time but that it is informal. Explain that you will not be present unless the group requests it, perhaps to answer a question. Tell them there will be no assessment and people can eat and drink if they like.
3 Make sure someone from the training team is on the premises during the group liaison time so that trainees can come and ask questions if they really need to. For the first couple of meetings it may be as well for a trainer to pop into the group meeting just to make sure that everyone is there, the task is understood and people are tackling it. This monitoring should be as light and non-interventionist as possible.
4 Explain to the group what you expect them to do with this time. If they have to teach lessons to the same class as each other, then they can use a task sheet such as that for guiding group liaison overleaf.

   If the time is to be used for language analysis and raising of trainees' awareness of points they are due to teach soon, then they may need guidance such as that provided by the language work task sheet also found overleaf.

   If the aim of the session is for participants to:
   - report on individual reading,
   - check they understand recent input,
   - plan an answer to an essay question, or
   - describe a recent lesson they've taught,

   then provide a detailed task sheet. Otherwise, the meeting can turn into a rather vague coffee break with people feeling they could have used the time better somewhere else.

### RATIONALE/COMMENT

a If the group liaison time is before a session, you will be able to start the session on time, with everyone present since the group liaison will have brought everyone together in one place. (This can be useful for first sessions on Monday morning!)
b This process encourages group formation and independence from the trainer.
c It allows time for important participant work which might otherwise get squeezed off the timetable or forgotten.

ACKNOWLEDGEMENT
Thanks to Mike Harding for the language task sheet.

## 7.10

**MATERIALS**
A task sheet (see page 180)

**TRAINEES**
Any

Example of a task sheet for groups of trainees who teach a class together: Group liaison time

Decide and/or confirm:
- who is teaching first, second, etc.,
- who will take charge of rounding up, greeting, settling, and saying goodbye to students,
- who will make/get/collect all the materials and photocopying you need,
- what is the *main aim* of the whole lesson and the different parts,
- which vocabulary, if any, needs to be pretaught.
- how you can link the warm-up to the rest of the lesson,
- how to guarantee a variety of learner constellations (e.g. whole group, pairs, etc.), pace and activity types,
- what language has recently been taught that could be recycled usefully,
- what pronunciation, word order, form or meaning problems you can expect and who is going to deal with them, not just at the presentation stage but throughout the lesson,
- who of the non-teachers will be doing which observation task.

© Longman Group UK Ltd 1992

### Example of language research task sheet: Using grammar books

Look at the following:
1 When he got home, his friends <u>had left</u>.
2 <u>She'll be going</u> to work now so why don't you get a lift with her?
3 Her father <u>made her work</u> very hard when she was a child.
4 The house <u>is being repainted</u> at the moment.
5 She lifted him up <u>so</u> he could see.
6 <u>Would you mind if</u> I stayed a bit longer?
7 <u>If I were you, I'd</u> stay till the end.

*Exercises:*
a Decide what structures the underlined words are examples of.
b Look up each structure in a grammar book and find out what use the example demonstrates. Do (a)–(b) with all seven examples before proceeding.
c When you have done the above, decide what kind of situation each example could be used in.
d Decide how you would encourage involvement from the students as you build up these situations and what prompts (for future use in drilling) you would try to elicit. Think of an activity or another situation which you could use to reactivate the language in later free extension.
e Work out what concept questions you would ask to check comprehension of each of the seven language items.

Do not go on to the last question until you have finished (a)–(e) for all of the examples.
f For 1–7, decide what you would use as your model sentence and how you would demonstrate the intonation/stress patterns.

© Longman Group UK Ltd 1992

# ADVICE: GIVING AND GETTING

## Procedure

1 Towards the end of a practical methodology course for trainees from different staffrooms, ask each trainee to think of three recent situations in which they've given advice to someone. The situations could be from their home, school or social life. The trainees jot down the three situations in note form.

2 Next, everybody notes down three situations in which advice was offered to them by someone else.

3 Ask the participants to assign a plus sign (+), a minus sign (−) or a question mark (?) to each situation. That is, if the advice was successfully communicated and accepted, trainees note down a plus sign. If it clearly wasn't, they note down a minus sign. If the outcome was doubtful, participants write a question mark.

4 Ask people to compare notes in small groups. What normally ensues is a discussion on the usefulness or otherwise of giving advice and how it feels to give and receive it.

### RATIONALE/COMMENT

It makes sense to give time towards the end of an in-service training course for participants to think about what they may want to share with their colleagues back home and when and how to do it. This process, and 7.12 *Yes, but . . .*, help trainees to foresee that colleagues back home may be a little resistant to the ideas and/or enthusiasm the prodigal brings home with them.

READING
Rinvolucri (1988).

**7.11**

MATERIALS
None

TRAINEES
Any from different staffrooms

TIMING
At the end of a course

# YES, BUT. . .

## Procedure

1 Towards the end of a practical methodology course with participants from different staffrooms, ask people to work in groups of four.

2 In just a few sentences, one person in each group tells the others about a problem they have at school.

3 The other three in the group offer advice to which the 'owner' of the problem replies with sentences starting, 'Yes, but . . .' and which go on to explain why the advice simply won't work. The rule in the exercise is that you have to reply, 'Yes, but . . .' even if you find the advice sensible and usable.

4 Each person in the groups of four has a go at presenting a problem and rejecting solutions by 'yes-butting'.

5 Come back into a plenary and get general feedback from the groups.

6 Discuss how the process relates to situations in trainees' own staffrooms.

**7.12**

MATERIALS
None

TRAINEES
Trainees about to return to their home schools where they will be working with other teachers

**RATIONALE/COMMENT**
As for 7.11 *Advice: Giving and getting*.

ACKNOWLEGEMENT/READING
I learnt this from Rick Cooper via Mario Rinvolucri. See Rinvolucri (1988).

## 7.13

**MATERIALS**
Envelopes and paper for letters

**TRAINEES**
Trainees about to finish a course

# A LETTER TO YOURSELF

## Procedure

1 At the end of a course, ask trainees to write a letter to themselves. The letters can contain reference to their experience of the course, what they feel they've learnt, where their expectations were fulfilled or disappointed and what they hope to do in future. Write a letter to yourself too.
2 When everyone has had time to write a letter, they should put it in an envelope marked with a contact address for six months ahead.
3 Take the letters in and hold on to them for the stipulated time. Then post them to the participants.
4 The next step could be to ask the trainees to write to you, themselves or each other a further letter containing the thoughts they have about the course now that it is long past and also their thoughts about their first letter.

**RATIONALE/COMMENT**
a There is a tendency for people to forget a course quickly when they return to a normally busy life. A letter from oneself, received well after the course is over, can be a reminder of the experience.
b Feedback conducted on the last day can be too soon for some impressions to be recorded. A participant receiving their own letter much later may be surprised how their feelings have changed in the interim. Realising this may lead participants to view feedback on their own courses differently.

# Bibliography

Aiello A, Argondizzo C and Romiti R 1987 The DTFM Course: how to humanize it. *English in School: Teacher Education* The British Council 1986 Sorrento Conference Report. The British Council/Modern English Publications

Allwright D 1984 Poster Presentation *TESOL Newsletter* **18**(3)

Allwright D 1988 *Observation in the Language Classroom* Longman

Baudains R and M 1990 *Alternatives* Longman

Beard R, Hartley J 1984 *Teaching and Learning in Higher Education* (4th edn) Harper and Row

Berer M, Rinvolucri M 1981 *Mazes* Heinemann Educational

Bligh D 1972 *What's the Use of Lectures?* Penguin

Bligh D, Jaques D and Warren-Piper D 1975 *Seven Decisions when Teaching Students* Exeter University Teaching Services

Bolitho R 1979 On demonstration lessons. Holden 1986. Teaching, teacher training and applied linguistics *The Teacher Trainer* **2**(3)

Bolitho R and Wajnryb R 1990 Being seen: in defence of demo lessons *The Teacher Trainer* **4**(1)

Bradbury P His quizzes are reprinted in Brown (1978). Originally done for the North East London Polytechnic Student Feedback Project

British Council 1985 *The Report of the British Council 1985 Bologna Conference* Modern English Publications

Britten D 1985 State of the art: Teaching training in higher education *Language Teaching* **18**(2) and (3)

Brown G 1978 *Lecturing and Explaining* Methuen

Brown G 1979 *Learning from Lectures* University of Nottingham

Brumfit C 1979 Integrating theory and practice. In Holden

Buzan T 1974 *Use Your Head* BBC Publications

Carmichael J 1987 The foreign language lesson – the trainees prepare the demonstration *The Teacher Trainer* **1**(2)

Cranmer D 1988 Learner, teacher or trainer? *The Teacher Trainer* **2**(2)

Crystal D 1985 *Dictionary of Linguistics and Phonetics* Basil Blackwell

Curran C 1972 *Counselling Learning: A Whole Person Model for Education* Apple River Press

Curran C 1976 *Counselling Learning in Second Languages* Apple River Press

Davis R (ed) 1979 *RSA Cert. TEFL Courses: Teacher Training Techniques and Problem Areas* Hilderstone College (St Peters Rd, Broadstairs, Kent, UK)

Davis P and Rinvolucri M 1988 *Dictation* Cambridge University Press

Deller S 1987 Observing and being observed *The Teacher Trainer* **1**(1)

Deller S 1990 *Lessons from the Learner* Longman

Dufeu B Forthcoming title Oxford University Press

Evans C 1988 *Language People: The Experience of Teaching and Learning Modern Languages in British Universities* Open University Press

Farthing J 1981 *Business Mazes* Hart-Davis Educational

Frank C and Rinvolucri M 1983 *Grammar in Action* Pergamon Press

Freeman D 1982 Observing teachers: three approaches to in-service training and development *TESOL Quarterly* **16**(1)

Fried-Booth D 1986 *Project Work* Oxford University Press

Gebhard J 1984 Models of supervision: choices *TESOL Quarterly* **18**(3)

Gibbs G 1981 *Teaching Students to Learn* Open University Press

Gibbs G, Habeshaw S and Habeshaw S 1984 *53 Interesting Ways to Assess Your Students* Technical and Educational Services

Goffman E 1971 *The Presentation of Self in Everyday Life* Penguin

Golebiowska A 1985 Once a teacher always a teacher *ELTJ*, **39**(4)

Gordon T 1974 *T.E.T.: Teacher Effectiveness Training* Peter Wyden

Haill A 1990 Writing as a learning processs in teacher education and development *The Teacher Trainer* **4**(1)

Harmer J 1983 *The Practice of English Language Teaching* Longman

Hawley R 1974 *Value Exploration through Role Playing* Education Resources, Massachussetts

Heron J 1974 *Co-Counselling* Human Potential Research Project, Department of Adult Education, The University of Surrey

Hess N 1987 The interview as a teacher training tool *The Teacher Trainer* **1**(3)

Hess N 1989 The flexible list *The Teacher Trainer* **3**(2)

Hess N 1991 *Headstarts* Longman

Holden S (ed) 1979 *Teacher Training* Modern English Publications

Hulbert J 1986 (Feb.) Case of conclusions or confusions *EFL Gazette*

Hundleby S, Breet F 1988 Using methodology notebooks on in-service teacher-training courses *ELTJ* **42**(1)

Jones R G (no date given) *Groundwork of Worship and Preaching* Epworth Press

Jordan R 1983 *Case Studies in ELT* Collins

Kenny G 1986a The teacher homework technique *The Teacher Trainer* **0**(0)

Kenny G 1986b Teacher homework *Practical English Teaching* **7**(1)

Lavery M 1988 Teaching people about themselves *The Teacher Trainer* **2**(2)

Lemke J 1989 *Using Language in the Classroom* Oxford University Press

Leutz G 1985 *Metre sa vie en scene* Edited and translated by B Dufeu. Desclée de Brouvver

Lindstromberg S (ed) 1990 *The Recipe Book* Longman

Maingay P 1987 Observation and feedback *The Teacher Trainer* **1**(3)

McLeish J 1976 The Lecture Method. In Gage U (ed) *The Psychology of Teaching Method* 75th yearbook of the National Society for the Study of Education, Chicago

Marks J 1989 Poster presentations, *The Teacher Trainer* **3**(3)

Moskowitz G 1978 *Caring and Sharing in the Foreign Language Classroom* Newbury House

Mugglestone P 1979 Mirroring classroom procedures. In Holden

Nin A 1966–1980 *The Journals of Anaïs Nin* Vols 1–7 Peter Owen

Open University Development Resource Team 1979 *The Language Curriculum* Open University Press

Peseschkian N 1986. *Oriental Stories as Tools in Psychotherapy* Springer Verlag

Plomer W (ed) 1960 *Kilvert's Diary* Vols 1–3 Penguin

Poynton C 1989 *Language and Gender* Oxford University Press

Progoff I 1978 *At a Journal Workshop* New York: Dialog House Library

Rinvolucri M 1985 Teacher Training Techniques *The Bologna Conference 1985 Report* Modern English Publications

Rinvolucri M 1987 A useful psychodrama model? *The Teacher Trainer* **1**(1)

Rinvolucri M 1988 Preparing in-service trainees for the return to their staffrooms after a practical methodology course *The Teacher Trainer* **2**(2)

Rinvolucri M 1989 The fishbowl *TESOL Greece Newsletter*, June

Rodgers A 1986 *Teaching Adults* Open University Press

Rosen S (ed) 1982 *My Voice Will Go with You* Norton

Rushton L 1987 Little boxes observation sheet *The Teacher Trainer* **1**(2)

Stevick E 1986 *Images and Options in the Language Classroom* Cambridge University Press

Sturtridge G 1987 Using posters in teacher education *The Teacher Trainer* **1**(2)

Taylor C 1988 *The Art and Science of Lecture Demonstration* Hilger

Tomlinson P 1988 Enhancing classroom skills: the radio assisted practice project (RAP) *The Teacher Trainer* **2**(1)

University Associates (Various materials for values clarification activities: 8517 Production Ave, PO Box 262401, San Diego, CA, USA)

UTMU (University of London Teaching Methods Unit) 1976 *Improving Teaching in Higher Education*

Verner C, Dickinson G 1968 The Lecture: an analysis and review of research *Adult Education* **17** winter

Wajnryb R 1990 Being seen *The Teacher Trainer* **4**(1)

Walker S 1988 Dealing with EFL terminology *The Teacher Trainer* **2**(2)

Weintraub E 1989 Interview in *The Teacher Trainer* **3**(1)

Wilberg P 1987 *One to One: A Teacher's Handbook* Language Teaching Publications

Woodward T 1987a The jargon generator *The Teacher Trainer* **1**(2)

Woodward T 1987b The discussion scales lecture *The Teacher Trainer* **1**(2)

Woodward T 1987c The Curran-style lecture *The Teacher Trainer* **1**(2)

Woodward T 1987d The buzz-group lecture *The Teacher Trainer* **1**(3)

Woodward T 1987e Flying visits *Modern Language Teacher's Journal* Sept

Woodward T 1988a *Loop Input* Pilgrims

Woodward T 1988b The starter question circle *The Teacher Trainer* **4092**(1)

Woodward T 1988c Taking the stress out of discussing lessons: an option-based approach *TESOL France News* summer

Woodward T 1988d Short practical ideas *The Teacher Trainer* **2**(3)

Woodward T 1988e The mind-map lecture *The Teacher Trainer* **2**(3)

Woodward T 1988f Splitting the atom *English Teaching Forum* **26**(4)

Woodward T 1989a Observation and feedback *The Teacher Trainer* **3**(1)

Woodward T 1989b Taping yourself *The Language Teacher* **2**(1) Language institute of Ireland

Woodward T 1989c Styles of EFL Teacher Trainer Input *System* **17**(1)

Woodward T 1989d Mapping the day *The Teacher Trainer* **3**(2)

Woodward T 1989e Component questions *PET* **10**(2)

Woodward T 1990 *Process in EFL Teacher Training* Unpublished M. Phil. dissertation, University of Exeter

Woodward T 1991 *Models and Metaphors in Language Teacher Training* Cambridge University Press

Wright A 1988 Some notes on giving talks at conferences *The Teacher Trainer* **2**(2)